# Mauritius

*Text by* Katerina Roberts
*Principal photographer:* Eric Roberts
*Edited by* John Mapps
*Design:* Roger Williams
*Series Editor:* Tony Halliday

**Berlitz** POCKET GUIDE

# Mauritius

*First Edition 2006*
*Updated 2007*

**NO** part of this book may be reproduced, stored in a retrieval system or transmitted in any form or means electronic, mechanical, photocopying, recording or otherwise, without prior written permission from Berlitz Publishing. Brief text quotations with use of photographs are exempted for book review purposes only.

**PHOTOGRAPHY CREDITS**
Eric Roberts 10, 11, 22, 27, 28, 30, 31, 32, 33, 38, 39, 41, 45, 46, 47, 49, 51, 54, 56, 58, 61, 63, 65, 66, 69, 71, 73, 74, 77, 78, 79, 80, 83, 84, 85, 86, 87, 88, 91, 93, 97, 99, 101, 103; Mauritius Tourism Promotion Authority 6, 7, 9, 20, 25, 34–5, 36, 42, 43, 90, 100; courtesy L'Aventure de Sucre Museum 95, 96, 104; age fotostock/SuperStock 53
Cover picture: Sylvain Grandadam/Robert Harding/Alamy

**CONTACTING THE EDITORS**
Every effort has been made to provide accurate information in this publication, but changes are inevitable. The publisher cannot be responsible for any resulting loss, inconvenience or injury. We would appreciate it if readers would call our attention to any errors or outdated information by contacting Berlitz Publishing, PO Box 7910, London SE1 1WE, England. Fax: (44) 20 7403 0290;
e-mail: berlitz@apaguide.co.uk
www.berlitzpublishing.com

*All Rights Reserved*

© 2007 Apa Publications GmbH & Co. Verlag KG, Singapore Branch, Singapore

*Printed in Singapore by Insight Print Services (Pte) Ltd, 38 Joo Koon Road, Singapore 628990.*
*Tel: (65) 6865-1600. Fax: (65) 6861-6438*

*Berlitz Trademark Reg. U.S. Patent Office and other countries. Marca Registrada*

►
Sugar island heritage: L'Aventure de Sucre Museum (page 42)

The forests and trails of the Domaine du Chasseur reserve (page 47) beckon nature-lovers

◄

The handsome Eureka mansion (page 33) is a colonial gem in a tropical garden setting
▼

# TOP TEN ATTRACTIONS

Huge waves crash against a wild coast at Le Gris Gris (page 55)

Arrive early for the vibrant Port Mathurin market (page 71), on the island of Rodrigues

Dramatic mountain vistas unfold in the forested Black River Gorges National Park (page 49)

Belle Mare beach (page 43) is the stuff of daydreams: white sand, palm trees and warm, turquoise waters

The Chamarel Waterfalls (page 51) tumble from the Black River Mountains

Clear waters, as at Île aux Cerfs (page 44), make for great snorkelling

Sir Seewoosagur Ramgoolam Botanic Gardens (page 41) showcase tropical plants

# CONTENTS

## Fact Sheets

# INTRODUCTION

Mauritius has long entranced its visitors. Charles Baudelaire called it 'the perfumed land, fondled by the sun', while Mark Twain noted simply that 'heaven was copied after Mauritius'. The stunning white, sandy beaches lapped by aquamarine seas earn every superlative, and thousands of modern visitors to Mauritius agree that this tiny dot in the Indian Ocean is the stuff of desert-island dreams. With much of its coastline fringed by coral reef, a landscape set off by diminutive mountains, temperatures rarely falling below 20°C (68°F) and some of the world's finest hotels, Mauritius is a perfect year-round holiday destination.

But there is more to Mauritius than the exclusive beachside hotels that have become the regular haunt of celebrities and big-spenders. Stray inland and you discover mountains, forests, rivers and waterfalls, undulating fields covered in sugar cane, extinct volcanic craters, tumbledown towns and villages, and good-natured locals.

**Dramatic Rempart Mountain**

Mauritius lies 805km (500 miles) east of Madagascar, one of a trio of islands, along with Rodrigues and Réunion, known as the Mascarenes. Shaped like a pear, Mauritius covers an area of 1,865 sq km (720 sq miles). The island forms the main component of the Republic of Mauritius, which also includes the much smaller islands of Agalega and St Brandon in the Carados Carajos group and the semi-autonomous island of Rodrigues.

There are three mountain ranges, courtesy of a volcanic past: the Moka range forms an amphitheatre around the capital Port Louis; the Black River chain occupies the southwest, merging with the Savanne mountains in the extreme south; and the Grand Port range lies in the southeast. Along the coast, the beaches, resorts and hotels of the north attract the majority of visitors; the west, with its fantastic sunsets and access to rugged inland areas, is fast catching up; the east is isolated and rural, but has some very luxurious hotels; the remote south is in the early stages of development.

## The People

There are no indigenous people. The 1.2 million islanders are the descendants of African slaves, indentured Indian labourers and Chinese traders, resulting in all shades of skin colour, a living legacy of over 300 years of colonisation by

---

### Creole

Creole is a language that was originally created by the need for French plantation masters to communicate with their slaves, and for the slaves, who often spoke different dialects, to understand each other. Creole became the island's *lingua franca*. Continuously modified by years of French and English colonisation, Indian immigration and Chinese settlers, it has become a hopelessly corrupted language that often confuses Mauritians themselves. Full of imagery and nuances, it is slightly easier to understand if you have a basic knowledge of French.

As a visitor staying in the tourist resorts you will get by without any difficulty speaking English or French, but in informal situations a few Creole expressions, such as *li bon* (that's good/fine) or *ki maniere* (how are you) or *tout correk* (OK), are always appreciated. If you're in Mauritian company, you'll find that the conversation may take place in Creole, French or English or a combination of all three.

the French and British. On
this, one of the most densely
populated islands on Earth,
Indo-Mauritians form the
majority at 68 percent, followed by Creoles or people
of mixed European or
African origin at 27 percent,
Sino-Mauritians at 3 percent
and white Franco-Maur-
itians at 2 percent. In Rodrigues there are only 37,000
islanders, mainly of Creole-

**A Mauritian smile**

African descent. For most of the time the republic's multicultural inhabitants get along in remarkable harmony.

Travelling round Mauritius reveals a naturally friendly people who are keen to help visitors. Many live in the crowded
plateau towns of Curepipe, Floreal, Rose Hill–Beau Bassin,
and Quatre Bornes in the centre of the island and in small villages. It is here that you discover the islanders' strong adher-
ence to cultural traditions, witness religious festivals, taste a
cuisine as diverse as its people and hear a multitude of different languages, including Creole, French, Hindi, Bhojpuri and,
to a lesser degree, English, in an environment that contrasts so
strongly with the luxurious beach hotels and bustling tourist
resorts of Grand Baie, Pereybere and Flic-en-Flac.

## Flora and Fauna

Three hundred years of human settlement has greatly altered
the vegetation and wildlife of Mauritius. Little remains of the
original flora other than a few patches of forest, declared as
nature reserves, in the centre of the island and on some off-
shore islands. The demise of the dodo in the 17th century *(see
page 15)* is only the most publicised extinction of the island's

**The masked weaver**

birdlife. Now only seven species of endemic birds remain, the most noted being the Mauritius kestrel, the pink pigeon and the echo parakeet. These birds can be seen in the Black River Gorges, while the pink pigeon now thrives on Île aux Aigrettes Nature Reserve off Mahebourg.

Imported fauna include deer, monkey, the tendrec (a sort of tail-less hedgehog), mongoose and the wild boar. There are three species of gecko, several tree lizards and the couleuvre, a non-poisonous snake from India. Wildlife is generally harmless, although extra care should be taken to avoid stepping on stonefish, whose spines can inflict serious injury.

## Sugar, Tourism and Beyond

Many fruits and vegetables and small amounts of coffee are grown for home consumption, although rice, a staple food, has to be imported in large quantities from Asia. Sugar cane is the dominant crop. Great tracts of it swathe the island, giving the land a fresh, green tropical appearance virtually year round.

Sugar production, once the island's most important industry, has given way to tourism and textile manufacturing, bringing Mauritius much-needed foreign income. While the impact of international terrorism and weather phenomena in Asia has, so far, had little effect on tourist numbers, increasing competition and a fall in demand resulted in the closure of many textile factories in 2004. In spite of this setback, economic diversification continues. Mauritius promotes itself as an offshore banking centre; a stock exchange was established in 1989; and a scheme to transform Mauritius into a 'cyber island' is almost complete, with the construction of several centres of business process outsourcing occupied by major foreign companies.

Mauritius is taking its first steps into 'green tourism'. Inland activities, such as rock-climbing, soft safaris, hiking, nature walks, quad-biking, canyoning and mountain-biking are now available for the first time in areas owned by sugar estates. Such excursions make a welcome change from the beach, revealing another face of this multi-faceted island. Luxury spa and golf resorts and eco-lodges, particularly on the fast-developing south coast, continue to grow. These new ventures, together with a surge in more affordable accommodation elsewhere and the introduction of charter flights, make the island more than just a holiday dream.

**The vibrant red of the flame tree**

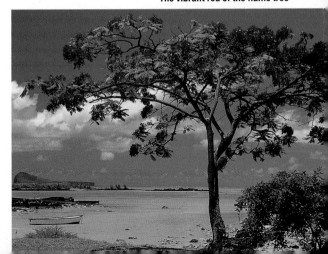

# A BRIEF HISTORY

Eight million years ago, Mauritius rose from the depths of the southwestern Indian Ocean in a series of volcanic eruptions. Réunion and Rodrigues followed a couple of million years later. These three islands are today known as the Mascarenes, after Portuguese Admiral, Pedro Mascarenhas, who visited the area in 1513.

The volcanic activity carved out a distinctive landscape of mountains, craters and coastal plains; lagoons and reefs were later additions. Trees and other plant life gradually covered the Mascarenes, which became the exclusive preserve of millions of birds attracted to a sea teeming with marine life. Prominent bird species included the flightless dodo of Mauritius and the solitaire of Rodrigues. Human occupation was to lead to the extinction of these species and the decimation of indigenous forests.

## Early Settlers

Early 15th-century Arab maps show Mauritius as Dina Arobi and Rodrigues as Dina Moraze, but there is no evidence that Arab explorers ever settled on either island. The first European visitors were the Portuguese in the early 16th century, who named Rodrigues after the navigator, Diego Rodriguez, and christened Mauritius after his ship the *Cirne*, Ilha do Cirne. Later Portuguese explorers and traders used the islands as convenient bases on the long voyages between the Cape of Good Hope and India but, like the Arabs, they never settled. They did leave a lasting legacy, however, by deliberately introducing cattle and monkeys so that there would be fresh meat supplies when ships called. These introduced animals, including rats and dogs escaping from ships, upset the delicate ecological balance that had existed for millions of years. In about 1539 the last Portuguese sailors left Mauritius and the island was unoccupied for over 50 years, save for occasional visits by pirates who roamed the Indian Ocean.

**Early 18th-century map**

## Arrival of the Dutch

The Dutch arrived in 1598, landing in the southeast of Mauritius at Vieux Grand Port, a natural harbour near present-day Mahebourg, and named the island after Prince Maurice of Nassau. They built a fort, the remains of which were excavated in 1997, and settled along the coast where they planted crops – including sugar cane – and began to cut down the ebony forests for export. With the French and British vying for this valuable commodity, the settlers realised that the harbour in the northwest was vulnerable to invasion and sent a small detachment of troops to what is the present capital, Port Louis. But cyclone, drought, food shortages and quarrels among settlers led to a Dutch withdrawal from the island in 1658.

In 1664 another attempt at colonisation was made when the Dutch East Indies Company, based in Batavia (present-day Jakarta, Indonesia) realised the strategic importance of Mauritius in the context of the sea route between Europe and the Indies. The new settlers cleared more ebony forests, introduced deer to overcome food shortages and imported slaves

**The doomed dodo, with the Grand Port mountain range behind**

from Madagascar and convicts from southeast Asia to work the fields. But apathy, an overall inefficient administration and attacks by pirates forced them to leave the island for good in 1710. All that was left was a group of runaway slaves. The only humans who came ashore were crews of visiting ships, and pirates who had established their own republic, Libertalia, in Madagascar in 1685. The pirates targeted the expanding maritime trade route between Europe and the Indies, raiding the ships of the various East India companies.

## French Colonisation

Soon after the Dutch left, the French arrived in 1715, took possession of the island and renamed it Île de France. The first French colonists landed at Mahebourg in 1722, but dangerous reefs and contrary winds threatened their ships, so they moved to the safety of Port Louis. Piracy continued throughout the French period. The French issued Letters of

Marque to pirates and owners of private ships, authorising them to attack foreign ships in the name of France. The holders of these letters became known as corsairs or privateers.

In 1735 Bertrand François Mahé de Labourdonnais, a naval officer, arrived at Port Louis as the new governor of the Mascarene Islands and set about transforming Île de France into a flourishing colony. A large labour force was crucial to his plans, and he began the importation of thousands of slaves from Africa and Madagascar. Ships were built, farms improved, roads constructed, and forests cut down to make way for sugar plantations. With French supremacy now well established in the Indian Ocean, the French East India Company supplied ships and stores to Port Louis for campaigns against the British in India.

In 1767 the company suffered heavy financial losses following the defeat of the French by the British in India. Labourdonnais was falsely accused of bribery and thrown into prison; Île de France was handed over to the crown. The French Revolution of 1789 had little effect on the islanders and if anything the influence of new ideas manifested itself

## The Demise of the Dodo

Mauritius' best-known indigenous bird, the dodo, is the world's most famous example of extinction and a symbol of man's destructiveness. The bird was fat, friendly and flightless. Clumsy and tame to the point of foolishness, this 23kg (50lb) bird made easy prey for the first Dutch settlers when they arrived in the early 17th century; they killed thousands of dodos for their meat. At the same time, the bird's eggs and chicks made tasty morsels for introduced animals, such as rats, monkeys and dogs. Some live dodos were taken to Europe and shown off as the greatest living freaks of the day. By the late 17th century, however, there were no more dodos to show off – the species had become extinct.

in a wave of loose living. The elite, bound by their common belief in slavery, had their own revolution when in 1796, France sent two officials to announce the news that slavery would be abolished. The colonists' fervour for liberty, equality and fraternity wore thin and the officials, amid rioting and unrest, were promptly sent back home.

Conflict with the British intensified, with the French using corsairs to attack British shipping. Between 1793 and 1802, corsairs captured more than a hundred East India ships, which were brought to Port Louis. The capital soon earned a reputation as a den of thieves where ruined adventurers, swindlers and pirates provided the corsairs with a ready outlet to dispose of stolen goods.

Île de France's period of autonomy lasted till 1803 when Napoleon appointed a new governor, General Decaen. Decaen curried favour with the elite by allowing slavery and privateering, both hugely profitable, to continue. Meanwhile, the British continued to lose valuable cargoes to the corsairs.

## British Colonisation

After months of blockading Port Louis, the British based themselves at Rodrigues and took Réunion before launching a major naval attack in 1810 on Mahebourg. The four-day Battle of Grand Port ended in defeat for the British, with heavy casualties on both sides. However, a few months later, in December, a huge British fleet landed at Cap Malheureux and troops marched to Port Louis. The French offered only token resistance and Île de France became a British colony, reverting to its former name, Mauritius.

**The Battle of Grand Port was the only French victory over the British at sea during the Napoleonic Wars. The battle is inscribed on the Arc de Triomphe in Paris.**

The capitulation terms were generous; anybody who wanted to leave could do so and were given a free passage home; settlers were allowed to keep their laws, customs, language, religion and property, which included their slaves. By eliminating Mauritius as a corsair base and establishing a governor and garrison, the British achieved supremacy in the Indian Ocean. English became the official language, but the island retained much of its French character.

Pont Etienne by Thuillier, 1847

Under Robert Farquhar, first British governor, Port Louis became a free port, roads were built and trade flourished. Sugar production soared and the planters badly needed slaves to clear land and plant cane – despite the fact that slavery had been abolished in the British Empire in 1807. In 1832 Judge John Jeremie, the Attorney-General, arrived in Mauritius to announce abolition without compensation to hostile planters and slave owners. He was forced to leave almost immediately. In response, the British built Fort Adelaide (La Citadelle) on a hill overlooking Port Louis to quell demonstrations. Slavery was finally abolished in 1835.

Britain turned to the Indian subcontinent for cheap labour to maintain sugar production. During the 19th century, nearly half a million Indians arrived at the Aapravasi Ghat in Port Louis, many in conditions not far

**Shops in 19th-century Port Louis, by Thuillier**

short of slavery. They were paid a pittance, worked long hours and often subjected to harsh treatment.

In 1872 a Royal Commission was appointed to look into the problems of Indian immigration. The Indians' living standards improved slightly and immigration was finally halted in 1909, when another Royal Commission made recommendations for social and political reform. By now many Indians had settled in Mauritius; today their descendants form the majority of the population.

In 1936 the Indians took political action and campaigned for better working conditions. Strikes the following year and again in 1943 brought the sugar industry to a standstill. The British responded by drawing up plans for constitutional reform. But the real turning point came in 1959 when the first elections under universal suffrage were held. They were won by the Labour Party under a Hindu doctor, Seewoosagur Ramgoolam (who was later knighted).

# Independence

In 1968 Britain agreed to grant independence on condition that the British take over the Chagos Archipelago, a group of islands 1,930km (1,200 miles) northeast of Mauritius. These islands, inhabited by the *ilois* or islanders, had been part of the British colony of Mauritius since 1814, when France ceded them to Britain. In 1965, a secret deal was made between Britain and the United States whereby in exchange for leasing one of the islands in the group, Diego Garcia, for 50 years, the British Government would get a discount of $11 million on Polaris submarines. The islands were then detached from Mauritius and became part of the new British Indian Ocean Territory (BIOT). The *ilois* were displaced and taken to Mauritius where they were dumped at the docks and left to fend for themselves. Diego Garcia is now a major US military base, off limits to all. Whether the *ilois* will ever return to their homeland seems nothing but a distant dream.

In the run-up to independence fears arose that politics would become 'Indianised', and many Mauritians settled abroad. In 1968 Sir Seewoosagur Ramgoolam became the first prime minister.

In the early 1980s, following a series of corruption scandals, high unemployment and over-population problems, the opposition party, the MMM, swept into power. Since then governments have been a coalition of all four major parties.

In 1992 Mauritius became an independent republic within the Commonwealth. The Queen was replaced as head of state by a locally nominated president.

**Sir Seewoosagur Ramgoolam (1900–85), the first prime minister of Mauritius, became known as 'the Father of the Nation'. The Royal Botanic Gardens at Pamplemousses were renamed in his honour in 1987.**

## Modern Mauritius

Since independence, the island's dependence on sugar has lessened. Manufacturing and textile industries rose in importance from the 1970s, but today the country's main markets for manufactured goods are turning to cheaper sources in China and India. Many textile factories have closed and unemployment is around 10 percent.

Sugar production, while still a major pillar of the economy, no longer employs the huge numbers it used to. Future changes to international sugar pricing agreements will hit the industry hard, and sugar barons are turning their lands over to real-estate development and tourism.

Tourism remains a major foreign income earner. New developments include the opening of luxurious golf and spa resorts on the south coast, and 'green tourism' activities, an attempt by the industry to show visitors another facet of the island, beyond the sea and beaches.

'Paradise Island' it may be for those who come for the magnificent beaches, but it may not be too long before Mauritius is better known as Cyber Island. In 2005 the country launched itself into information and communications technology with the opening of Cyber City. This complex in the centre of the island, the result of Indian expertise and financial backing, has already attracted foreign companies involved in call centres and business process outsourcing. New jobs are being created to replace those lost in other sectors. Only time will tell if this ambitious scheme can succeed.

**Facing the future head on**

# Historical Landmarks

**15th century** Arab names of Dina Arobi and Dina Moraze for Mauritius and Rodrigues appear on early maps.

**1513** The Mascarene Islands are named after Portuguese navigator, Pedro Mascarenhas.

**1528** Diego Rodriguez, Portuguese seaman, visits Rodrigues and gives the island his name.

**1598** First Dutch landing at Port South East.

**1638–1710** Dutch settle in Mauritius but abandon it after several attempts to colonise. First slaves imported from Madagascar. Sugar cane, deer, pigs from Java introduced.

**1691–93** Rodrigues first settled by François Leguat and nine others.

**1715** French annex Mauritius, naming it Île de France.

**1721–1810** French occupation. Slaves imported in huge numbers.

**1735** Labourdonnais becomes first governor of the Mascarene Islands.

**1793–1805** Privateering causes large losses to British East India Company. French Revolution and Napoleonic Wars provoke revolutionary fervour in Mauritius.

**1810** British take Île de France and rename it Mauritius.

**1814** The Treaty of Paris places Mauritius, Rodrigues and the Seychelles under British ownership; Réunion is handed back to the French.

**1835** Slavery abolished and replaced by Indian indentured labour.

**1909** Indian immigration ceases. Royal Commission appointed to make recommendations for political and social reform.

**1936** Labour Party formed.

**1968** Independence from Britain. Rodrigues becomes a dependency of Mauritius. Sir Seewoosagur Ramgoolam is prime minister.

**1982** Sir Seewoosagur Ramgoolam defeated in general election.

**1992** Republic of Mauritius declared.

**2002** Rodrigues granted regional autonomy.

**2005** Opening of Cyber Tower I at Ebene; Navin Ramgoolam of the Social Alliance elected prime minister.

**2006** Aapravasi Ghat becomes UNESCO World Heritage Site.

# WHERE TO GO

This guide divides Mauritius into bite-size geographical chunks. Port Louis, the capital, and the plateau towns are worth a visit at least once to experience contemporary island life. The north coast (the northwest in particular) is home to the most established resorts. The more isolated east coast may be too windy for some during the winter months, but the hotels here offer unadulterated luxury and access to some lovely offshore islands. The west coast, renowned for stunning sunsets, has fine diving and water sports and is within easy reach of the rugged Black River Gorges, as is the developing south coast. The little island of Rodrigues, a newcomer to tourism, offers a total contrast to Mauritius, with simple hotels, rugged landscapes and a predominantly Afro-Creole population.

## PORT LOUIS

In 1735 Bertrand François Mahé de Labourdonnais, the Governor-General of the Mascarene Islands, founded this settlement on the northwest coast. With 150,000 residents crammed into less than 10 sq km (4 sq miles) and thousands of workers who arrive daily from nearby, it's no surprise that Port Louis, like most capitals, is crowded, dirty and noisy. It is devoid of any real architectural wonders and makes no claim to urban chic, but its fascination lies in its jumble of Franco-British colonial buildings juxtaposed against modern office blocks and a hotchpotch of tumbledown shops and stores dwarfed by modern mini-skyscrapers.

Surrounding the city are the picturesque peaks and knolls of the Moka Mountains, including the distinct thumb-shaped

**Belle Mare public beach**

Le Pouce, the tapered pinnacle of Pieter Both, named after the Dutch admiral who drowned nearby, and the huge bulk of Signal Mountain to the south. It's an atmospheric city with statues and monuments shaded by palm trees, colourful Chinese and Indian temples and churches, and a bustling market and modern waterfront. The often debilitating summer humidity reminds you that you are in the tropics.

If you are heading from the airport to one of the archetypal beach hotels in the north, your first glimpse of the capital will be from the traffic-infested dual carriageway, locally referred to as the 'motorway', which divides the old commercial district from the waterfront. Every visitor should try to spend at least a morning exploring the back streets of Port Louis with its tiny 'hole in the wall' shops, bargaining in the market and eating on the hoof along with the lunchtime crowds. Apart from the Caudan Waterfront, it's not a city that stays awake after dark.

## The Waterfront

Built in 1996 to replace the old harbour, the pedestrianised **Caudan Waterfront** complex has become the focal point of

### The Mauritian Flag

Port Louis is at its most colourful on Independence Day, held on 12 March, when Government House and other public buildings are festooned with the national flag. The Mauritian flag consists of four horizontal coloured bands in red, blue, yellow and green. Officially red represents freedom and independence, blue is for the sea, yellow is for the lights of independence shining over the nation and green for the swathes of sugar cane that are so characteristic of the country. Others maintain that it reflects the island's multi-faith community: red is for the followers of Hinduism, blue for the Catholic community, yellow for the Tamils and green for the Muslims.

**The Caudan Waterfront**

the capital. Its two modern hotels, a 24-hour casino, designer boutiques, restaurants and businesses are housed in renovated coaster sheds and dockside buildings. In spite of recent developments, the sights of the harbour remind you that this is a working port: the industrial landscape of docks and quays includes the squat, solid red-brick Granary building (now a car park), the spruced-up Bulk Sugar Terminal, as well as cargo ships.

In 1847 Mauritius became the fifth country in the world to issue postage stamps *(see page 64)*; the very first stamps – the Mauritian Two Penny Blue and One Penny Orange-Red – are now extremely valuable. This philatelic history is on display to the south of the waterfront in the **Blue Penny Museum** (open Mon–Sat 10am–5pm; admission fee). The philately exhibits include examples of both stamps, and there are fine artworks, old maps, coins, postcards and historic photographs as well.

To the north, behind a smart arcade of souvenir shops, is the quirky **Windmill Museum** (open Mon–Fri 10am–noon, 1–3pm; free), which is a reconstruction of the original mill built by the French in the 18th century. Inside, a collection of old photographs of Port Louis shows the transformation of the waterfront, and there are some anchors and cannon found during the renovation works. A childrens' play area and mini-train ride provide distraction for young families.

Still on the waterfront and to the north is the colonnaded **Post Office**, built by the British in 1868, and the **Postal Museum** (open Mon–Fri 9am–3.45pm, Sat till 11.30am; free), which has a small collection of 19th-century telegraph and stamp-vending machines, postal stationery and printing plates. The museum is also a good place to buy first-day covers, commemorative stamps and other things of interest to philatelists.

Nearby are the gardens of the **Aapravasi Ghat**. This area used to be an immigration depot for the first indentured Indian labourers who arrived in 1834 to work on sugar estates in conditions not far from slavery. In 2006 Aapravasi Ghat was given UNESCO World Heritage Site status; it is recognised as the place where the 'modern indentured labour diaspora' began. Scenes of immigrant life are depicted on bronze murals.

> **Within a decade of the first immigrants from India in 1834, half a million more arrived, making Mauritius the biggest recipient of Indian labour in the British Empire and its most successful sugar-producing colony.**

## Old Port Louis

**Place d'Armes**, directly opposite the waterfront, is a good place to start a tour of Old Port Louis. Here the statue of Mahé de Labourdonnais stares out to sea. Shaded by an avenue of royal palms and flanked by banks and offices, this one-way street is the heart of the capital and Port Louis' busiest thoroughfare. At the end of the street is **Government House**, built on the site of a tumbledown wooden shack that was later enlarged by Labourdonnais as his headquarters when he transformed the city from an Indian Ocean backwater into a thriving sea port. A marble statue of Queen Victoria and, behind it, a statue of Sir William Stevenson, the British governor from 1857 to 1863, are reminders of the city's colonial past. To the right, on the corner of La Chaussée, are the former **Treasury Buildings** built in 1883, now the Prime Minister's Office, with large overhanging verandas providing respite from tropical downpours.

Along La Chaussée is the **Natural History Museum** (open Thur–Tues 9am–4pm; free), an attractive cream-coloured colonial building fronted by a huge baobab tree. The displays inside of a stuffed dodo, marine life and shells are

**Statue of Mahé de Labourdonnais in Place d'Armes**

**Company Gardens**

disappointing. Beyond the museum are **Company Gardens**, where the French East India Company had its headquarters. Today, with its bottle palms, giant banyans and statues of famous island sons, it is a pleasant sylvan lunchtime setting for office workers.

The **Municipal Theatre**, built in 1822 in Intendance Street, is the oldest theatre in the Indian Ocean. Its ornate interior includes an intricately painted domed ceiling, crystal chandeliers and seats in the gods.

Across the road and tucked down the cobbled lane of Rue de Vieux Conseil is the **Museum of Photography** (opening hours vary, tel: 211 1705; admission fee). It is crammed with impressive displays of late 19th-century photographic equipment, postcards and photographs of Port Louis.

City Hall and the adjacent government buildings are examples of the uninspiring concrete architecture of the 1960s, but you can't avoid them to get to the Roman Catholic **St Louis Cathedral** in Cathedral Square. This twin-towered neo-gothic cathedral, dating from 1932, is the third to be built on this site, both of its predecessors having been destroyed in cyclones. In the chapel are the remains of Madame Labourdonnais and her son. The fountain outside with its four bronze lions dates back to 1786 and provided water for city folk. Immediately behind the cathedral is the fine 19th-century colonnaded mansion of the **Episcopal Palace** with its high ceilings and wide verandas.

> **The walls of St James Anglican Cathedral were built 10ft (3m) thick to make them cyclone proof, allowing Port Louisiens to shelter inside when these fierce tropical storms struck.**

The cream-coloured Anglican **St James Cathedral**, hidden in tranquil Poudriere Street, occupies the site of a former gunpowder store where the French incarcerated British prisoners-of-war. The British built the present single-spired cathedral in 1828 and installed a bell, which had belonged to a French governor.

At the eastern edge of Port Louis and cradled by the Moka Mountains is the **Champs de Mars** racecourse, the oldest in the southern hemisphere, best seen from the heights of **La Citadelle**, a now abandoned basalt-built lookout post built to the north by the British in 1832. Under the French the area was a military training ground and in 1812 it was turned into a racecourse by Colonel Edward Draper, a British army officer. Fringing the north side in Dr Eugene Laurent Street is a colourful Chinese temple bedecked with ornate scripts. For respite from the heat, make for the walking trails at **Le Dauget** in the foothills of the Moka Mountains; there are panoramic views of the city and harbour.

After 160 years of providing Port Louisiens with fresh produce from a dilapidated site between Queen and Farquhar streets, the **Central Market** moved in 2003 into an adjacent clean and modern two-storey stone and timber building. All that remains of the old market are the Victorian wrought-iron gates and a drab meat and fish section. The new market (open daily), which has its main entrance in Queen Street, is worth visiting for its bustling atmosphere, brash colours, strange smells and unexpected sights. You can barter for baskets,

**The Jummah Mosque**

clothing, T-shirts, spices and even salt fish and honey, wend your way through the fruit and vegetable stalls, or buy a herbal remedy 'guaranteed to cure all ills' from happy-go-lucky traders. The ground floor is packed with fruit and vegetable sellers and there is an air-conditioned food section selling hygienically prepared snacks and drinks. The upper floor has a small eating area and great views of the market.

Perhaps the most eclectic part of the city is several blocks east of the market towards the pagoda-like entrance of **Chinatown**. The air is thick with the smell of herbs and spices and the streets bristle with specialist food shops, *ayurvedic* stores, small eateries and chaotic supermarkets. Standing sentinel on the corner of Jummah Mosque Street and Royal Road is the green and white **Jummah Mosque**. Built in 1853, it is the island's most impressive mosque, with ornate teak doors and decorative walls. If you ask permission, you may be allowed to visit the courtyard.

Three Chinese temples, open to the public, are some distance from Chinatown. The oldest is the **Kwan Tee Pagoda**, beside the busy roundabout south of the Caudan Waterfront, dedicated to the Chinese warrior god. Another, simply known as the **Chinese Pagoda**, is located on the corner of Generosity and Justice streets where the scent of sandalwood drifts from the red and gold interior. There is a Buddhist shrine on the first floor affording wonderful city views. The most serene is the cream-coloured **Thien Thane** temple in the verdant foothills of Signal Mountain on the southeast edge of town. Remember to remove your shoes when entering a temple.

Also on the foothills of Signal Mountain and a world away from the brouhaha of town is the peaceful setting of the shrine of **Marie Reine de la Paix**. In 1989 this place of pilgrimage was crammed with thousands of islanders gathered to hear mass said by Pope John Paul II. It is still used by the Catholic community for religious gatherings. From the wide paved walkway and lovely lawned terraces there are great views of the city and harbour.

**Line Barracks**, which has its public entrance in Jemmapes Street, sits squarely around a central courtyard and takes up several city blocks. Built in 1764 by the last governor of the French East India Company to house troops who had previously been billeted in private homes, today it is the headquarters of the Mauritius Police Force and is arguably one of Port Louis' quirkiest sites. Learner drivers take their licence test here, gingerly steering a course round gardens containing a petrified dodo and the odd cannon or two and past the city prison dubbed 'Alcatraz', before emerging into the busy streets through an incongruous blue-tiled archway marked 'Gateway of Discipline'.

**The Thien Thane temple**

**Stained glass in Père Laval**

## Outside Port Louis

The **Church and Shrine of Père Laval**, to the northeast of Port Louis in the suburb of Sainte-Croix, is dedicated to the French missionary, Jacques Desiré Laval, who arrived in 1841 to convert black ex-slaves to Catholicism. When Père Laval died in 1864, his special healing powers became legendary and in 1979 the Catholic Church beatified him. The modern white church replaced the original, which was damaged by Cyclone Carol in 1962, and is worth visiting for its abstract-style **stained-glass windows**, lofty convex timber ceiling and modern mosaics depicting the life of Christ. Beside the church stands a vault containing a stone sarcophagus enclosing the remains of Père Laval's body beneath an effigy framed with flowers and candles placed by people of all faiths. There is also a small shop selling postcards, books and souvenirs of a religious bent, and plenty of information in French and English on the life of Père Laval. The adjacent **presbytery** is a superb example of 19th-century colonial architecture.

South of the capital, just off the motorway at Pailles, is the 1,200-hectare (3,000-acre) estate of **Domaine les Pailles** (open daily 10am–5.30pm; admission fee). The estate includes a reconstruction of an early oxen-powered sugar mill, a spice garden, rum distillery and mask museum; there are optional guided tours. Rides in a colonial-style horse-drawn carriage, jeep safaris and activities for children are also offered. Four restaurants, one with a swimming pool *(see page 136)*, a casino and the futuristic-style **Swami**

**Vivekananda Conference Centre** make the estate a popular destination for both business people and tourists.

Further south along the motorway at Montagne Ory is the colonial mansion of **Eureka** (open daily 10am–4pm; admission fee). Built in 1856 by an Englishman, it was later auctioned to the wealthy Leclezio, a Franco-Mauritian family, one of whom cried 'Eureka' when his bid was accepted. This ancestral home is now a museum. Built entirely of indigenous wood, the main house has 109 doors, and the high-ceilinged rooms are filled with antique furniture that reflects a bygone era. You can take tea on the spacious veranda of the main house, lunch at the smaller annexe called Le Ravin, explore the external stone-built kitchen crammed with original Creole cookware or take a nature walk through tropical gardens towards a deep ravine and waterfall.

**Part of the Eureka estate**

## THE NORTH

The coast north from Port Louis attracts the most visitors to Mauritius because of the stunning stretches of white, sandy beaches backed by turquoise lagoons, the fine hotels, and the popular resorts of Trou aux Biches, Grand Baie and Pereybere. The region also has access to a collection of off-shore islands, as well as a number of inland attractions, providing distraction for beach lovers and water-sports enthusiasts. Although hotels maintain the best beaches, no beach is private and as long as you don't access them via the hotel entrance you are free to use them. A fast dual-lane carriageway, locally referred to as the 'motorway', links the

**Cap Malheureux church**

north to Port Louis, with a series of roundabouts leading to villages and on to the various resorts.

Inland, sugar cane clothes a flat landscape broken by the gentlest of hills. From July to December when the cane is harvested, there are superb views to the south of Port Louis' Moka Mountains, which provide a natural compass from which to get your bearings if you're walking, cycling or driving. At other times of the year, the sugar cane is so high that the view is obscured and travelling is like being in a maze, although there is always somebody around to ask for directions.

## North from Port Louis

A series of sheltered bays and long stretches of beach pepper the coast north of the capital. First is **Le Goulet**, an attractive white crescent of sand nestling between low cliffs and backed by a forest of casuarinas just off the Arsenal road. Next is the **Baie du Tombeau** (Bay of the Tombs) on the B29. In 1615 four ships belonging to the Dutch East India Company were caught in a cyclone, which swept them on to the reef here. Everybody drowned, including Admiral Pieter Both, after whom the Port Louis mountain peak is named.

The next bay is **Baie aux Tortues** (Turtle Bay), dominated by appealing beach hotels flanking the banks of the River Citron. Here, ammunition was supplied for French

**Hindu temples add to the local colour**

expeditions to India from an arsenal at nearby Moulin a Poudre. The bay is a designated marine park, its rich underwater life, including fabulous corals, making it perfect for snorkelling. At nearby Balaclava there are some ruins of a 19th-century private estate and a waterfall inside the grounds of the Maritim Hotel.

The small village of **Pointe aux Piments** hugs the shore, revealing glimpses of local life and a lovely rocky beach backed by grassy verges dotted with religious shrines. The modern **Aquarium** (open daily 9am–4pm; admission fee) on the coast road is worth visiting for its collection of reef and lagoon fish displayed in several huge tanks.

**Trou aux Biches**, a former fishing village, has developed into a low-key international resort with the hotel of the same name dominating 3km (2 miles) of a white, sandy beach. There's also a hotel casino and nine-hole golf course, a few tourist shops and small supermarkets. At nearby **Triolet** is the island's largest Hindu shrine, built in 1857, the imposing **Maheswarnath Temple**. In return for a guided tour, you may be asked for a donation, which you should place directly into the sealed box at the entrance.

The most popular public beach is further north at **Mon Choisy**. Here, a grassy football pitch, a former landing strip, is marked with a monument commemorating the first flight from Mauritius to Réunion in 1933 by two French pilots, Hily and Surtel. At weekends the blindingly white beach is crammed with campers in makeshift tents and families feasting on *farathas* and curries; impromptu *sega* dances take place beneath the shade of a dense casuarina forest. Midweek it is an ideal location for snorkelling, swimming, strolling or horse-riding. At the back of the beach, **Horse Riding Delights**, a former 19th-century sugar estate that is now a leisure park (tel: 265 6159, reservations only), offers guided tours of the ruins and an insight into how sugar shaped the economy of the island.

**Pointe aux Canonniers** (Gunners Point), reached through an avenue of flamboyant trees from Mon Choisy, is an historic headland. The French used it as a garrison and shore battery and the British as a military and quarantine post. Today, this is a tranquil coastline indented with pristine beaches, and the only surviving colonial remains are a 19th-century lighthouse and a few cannon in the grounds.

## Grand Baie

The appeal of Grand Baie, billed as the island's premier resort, lies in the profusion of shops, restaurants and cafés not attached to hotels strung around a deep turquoise bay dotted with plea-

The area now known as Pointe aux Canonniers was dubbed by early Dutch settlers De Vuyle Hoek (Filthy Corner) because so many of their ships were swept on to the reef.

sure craft. Called overrated by some islanders, who point to its lack of pavements, congested coast road, tatty tourist shops and night-time prostitution, Grand Baie for most European holidaymakers is heaven, thanks to its slow, easy-going atmosphere and range of hotels, apartments and self-catering accommodation mostly within walking distance of the action. The resort also draws people from all over the island for its Friday and Saturday nightlife, and many Mauritians have second homes here.

Centre of operations is Sunset Boulevard where designer shops rub shoulders with cafés, souvenir shops and the Sportfisher Big Game Fishing Centre. Tour operators line the street,

**La Cuvette in Grand Baie**

offering car and bicycle hire, excursions and trips to off-shore islands, plus all water-based activities, such as diving, water skiing, wind-surfing, parasailing, under-water safaris and undersea walks. For a swim, avoid the beach on the coast road and head to **La Cuvette** at the north of the bay. It has a parking area, showers, food kiosks and toilets, and you can swim beyond the basalt rocks on the right-hand side and onto the beach fronting the celebrity-starred Royal Palm Hotel.

## North from Grand Baie

Just 2km (1 mile) north of Grand Baie is **Pereybere**,

which offers affordable self-catering apartments, a fairly buzzing nightlife in bars and beach-fronted eateries, safe swimming and a handy bus route linking it with Port Louis. It is popular with independent travellers as an alternative to brash Grand Baie. At weekends, convoys of mobile food wagons, ice-cream vans and lorries crammed with picnicking

**Grand Gaube kiosk**

families from Port Louis liven up this normally quiet beach.

Shallow bays and rocky coves combine to make a picturesque 6-km (4-mile) journey north via Bain Boeuf to the island's most northerly point, **Cap Malheureux**. A pretty red-roofed church surrounded by grassy lawns overlooks the lagoon to the wedge-shaped island of Coin de Mire, directly opposite. In 1810 a massive British naval force anchored off its shores before marching to Port Louis to take possession of Mauritius.

More sparkling beaches backed by casuarina forests unfold at Anse la Raie, before the road hits the cane fields leading to **Grand Gaube**, a fishing hamlet fanned by north-east trade winds. A 2004 refurbishment programme included an upgraded public beach, a children's play area and neat coast road, yet the colourful tumbledown stores at the back of the village have lost none of their earthy charm.

South of Grand Gaube is the bustling town of **Goodlands** where a textiles and clothing market (Tuesday and Friday) attracts hundreds of locals and tourists. Directly opposite the market is the island's biggest model shipmakers, **Historic Marine** (open Mon–Fri 8am–5pm, Sat–Sun 9am–noon; free guided tour), where models based on original museum plans, and nautical furniture, are produced and sold.

To the southeast of Goodlands is **Poudre d'Or**, where an obelisk on the headland opposite the reef commemorates the sinking of the *St Geran* in 1744 and the drowning of a young engaged couple. The event inspired 18th-century writer, Bernadin de St Pierre, to pen the romantic Mauritian classic, *Paul et Virginie*, after whom a hotel at Grand Gaube is named. Some of the wreckage from the *St Geran* is displayed at Mahebourg's National History Museum *(see page 46)*. For a great day's snorkelling in translucent waters, local fishermen will ferry you to uninhabited **Île d'Ambre**, where early sailors found ambergris (a waxy substance secreted by sperm whales). For bracing walks along windy, deserted rock-studded beaches, head further south to isolated **Roches Noires**, but do not swim here because the currents are dangerous.

## Northern Offshore Islands

Operators in Grand Baie offer full-day tours with barbecue lunch to all the offshore islands, including Île aux Cerfs *(see page 44)* in the east and Île aux Benitiers *(see page 62)* in the west. Most popular for swimming and snorkelling are the reef-enclosed waters between **Flat Island** and **Gabriel Island**. On Flat Island, pathways, a lighthouse and cemetery bear testimony to those who died during the 1856 cholera epidemic, while the deserted beaches of Gabriel have changed little since the island's days as a quarantine post. Great views of the coast from the open sea make a cruise to **Coin de Mire** a wonderful day out, although going ashore here is not possible due to the island's crumbling volcanic rock. **Round Island** (which isn't round) is home to the rare Telfair skink and **Serpent Island** (which has no snakes) is a bird sanctuary. Both are designated nature reserves for which you need permission to enter.

## Pamplemousses and the Sugar Museum

The north's top attraction is the **Sir Seewoosagur Ramgoolam Botanic Gardens** (open daily 6am–6pm; free), formerly known as the Royal Botanic Gardens, at Pamplemousses. Well signposted on the motorway north of Port Louis, the gardens are only a 30-minute drive from Grand Baie. A visit makes a pleasant change from the coast. Official guides (fee payable) may offer to show you around the 25-hectare (62-acre) site, or you can wander at will. Mazes of shady palm-lined avenues border indigenous Mascarene island flora. Impressive sights include the graceful yellow and white lotus flowers of the Lotus Pond, and the huge, flan-case-shaped leaves of the giant Amazon water lilies in the Lily Pond. Other specimens include the curiously named marmalade box, chewing gum and sausage trees. In 1735, under Labourdonnais, the area was a market garden, which provided fresh supplies for ships calling at Port Louis.

Among the other notable sights are the white wrought-iron gates, which were exhibited at the Great Exhibition of 1851 at London's Crystal Palace. The imposing **Chateau de Mon Plaisir**, built in the mid-19th century by the British, was named after the original

**Giant Amazon water lilies in the botanic gardens**

**Mill wheels in L'Aventure de Sucre Museum**

chateau occupied by Pierre Poivre, the French Intendant and horticulturist who first introduced many of the species that grow here today. The gardens are earmarked for a major overhaul, which will attract an admission fee.

➤ **L'Aventure de Sucre Museum** (open daily 9am–6pm; admission fee), just 0.5km (¼ mile) from Pamplemousses at Beau Plan Sugar Estate, is a former sugar factory converted into a fascinating museum. You can easily spend half a day here exploring, with the aid of interactive displays, the history of sugar and its importance to the social and economic development of Mauritius. Original equipment includes huge mill wheels, evaporation tanks and an old sugar boat authentically anchored in a reconstructed indoor harbour. Guided tours are also available. There is a kids' corner with short films and cartoons, a shop selling speciality sugars and unusual souvenirs, plus the pleasant Fangourin restaurant.

# THE EAST

Some of the island's most luxurious hotels are located on the east coast, but this area remains essentially isolated and rural, an area of agricultural land, broken by vistas of picturesque mountains, slow-moving fishing villages and inviting beaches. Many hotels lie in sheltered positions, protected from the southeast trade winds that blow year round but are especially strong from May to November. Away from the beaches, there are some rewarding historic and scenic attractions to be explored. Getting around by public transport can be frustrating and it may be better to hire a car.

## Belle Mare to Île aux Cerfs

The main town is **Centre de Flacq**. There's not much to see here apart from the Sunday market, tumbledown shops and a 19th-century courthouse, but there are plenty of buses and taxis to other parts of the island. East of the town through flat cane fields is beautiful **Belle Mare public beach** lapped by an idyllic lagoon. Barbecue areas, the odd mobile food wagon and meandering paths through the casuarinas replace the straw parasols and swanky sophistication of the hotels flanking the beach, while old kilns testify to the former industry of coral burning. Nearby a monument commemorates the death of 159 passengers and crew whose South African Airways flight crashed in unexplained circumstances off the east coast in 1987. There are several champi-

**Parasols at Belle Mare beach**

onship golf courses in the area and children can enjoy the water chutes and slides at the nearby **Waterpark**.

South along the coast road, the small village of **Trou d'Eau Douce** has narrow streets, colourful tourist shops and simple restaurants. Tour operators provide a 10-minute ferry service from here to **Île aux Cerfs**. The island consists of 280 hectares (700 acres) of luxuriant woodland, an 18-hole golf course, two eateries and a few souvenir shops. You can wander along shaded paths, find deserted beaches, snorkel and swim, go parasailing, enjoy a barbecue lunch at uninhabited **Île Mangenie** or take a speed-boat trip to Mauritius's longest river, the boulder-strewn Grande Rivière Sud-Est, which terminates in cascading waterfalls at Beau Champ.

Heading south from Beau Champ, fields of sugar cane stretch towards the Bambous Mountains, which form a dramatic backdrop to the isolated fishing villages of Deux Freres, Quatre Souers and Grand Sable. The road hugs the shore until rising to **Pointe du Diable** (Devil's Point), a grassy headland, where Creole superstition credits the devil with upsetting the compasses of passing ships. Two cannon dating back to 1759 mark the site of a French battery, from whose ruined walls there are fine views of **Île aux Phares**. This was the island on which the Dutch imprisoned Rodrigues' first settler, François Leguat *(see pages 70 and 72)*, in 1693.

**Vieux Grand Port**, lying in the shadow of Lion Mountain, marks the beginning of an historic route along the coast. In 1598 the Dutch landed here, called it Warwyck Bay and built Fort Frederick Henry at the north of the town. It is now a collection of ruined walls with evidence of 18th-century French defences. The adjacent **Fort Frederick Henry Museum** (open Mon–Sat 9am–5pm, Sun 9am–noon; admission fee) contains a model of the original fort, artefacts unearthed during a 1997 archaeological dig, and audio-visual displays of the history of the Dutch East India Company in Mauritius.

Under the French, the area was renamed Port Bourbon and became the headquarters of the French East India Company, but the prevailing fierce southeast trade winds forced the company to move to Port Louis. Soldiers and sweethearts meanwhile would meet at **Bois des Amourettes** further north, the former maintaining their honour in duels fought in the sea caves at **Salles d'Armes** to the south. At **Ferney**, Dutch monuments commemorate the first landing in 1598 and the introduction of deer and sugar cane in 1639.

## Mahebourg to Blue Bay

Lying on the southern shores of the bay of Vieux Grand Port with views of Lion Mountain to the north is **Mahebourg**, named after Mahé de Labourdonnais. It is a laid-back village, which in spite of its bustling Monday market and dilapidated stores and shops, strives to maintain its colonial heritage: the

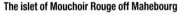

The islet of Mouchoir Rouge off Mahebourg

**The National History Museum**

streets, laid out in a grid pattern, are named after early European settlers; a **waterfront obelisk** facing the pretty islet of **Mouchoir Rouge** commemorates the Battle of Grand Port in 1810; an 18th-century washhouse called **Le Lavoir**, off Rue de la Passe, is still used as an outdoor laundry; and there's a quirky **boat-shaped monument** to Ferney-born journalist Remy Ollier, who represented the interests of the black population in the mid-19th century.

A short stroll north of the village is **Cavendish Bridge**, which crosses La Chaux River to **Ville Noire**, named after black slaves who arrived in appalling conditions to work the French-owned sugar plantations. Tucked around the back streets is the oldest factory in Mauritius, the **Rault Biscuit Factory** (open Mon–Fri 9–11am, 1–3pm; admission fee), where *biscuits manioc* are made from the cassava root. This family-run firm offers guided tours finishing with vanilla-flavoured tea and freshly baked biscuits. A scenic drive past the factory along the B7 through cane fields backed by the gorgeous Creole Mountains leads to **Riche en Eau**, where chimneys mark the site of early family-run sugar estates.

Mahebourg's **National History Museum** (open Wed–Mon 9am–4pm; free) is housed in a renovated colonial mansion on the A10 leading out of the village towards the airport. Built in 1722 and the former residence of a French dignitary, it was hastily turned into a makeshift hospital in 1810 where admirals of the French and British fleets convalesced following the three-day Battle of Grand Port *(see page 16)*.

The museum contains maps and documents from the Dutch, French and British colonial periods, a frieze of the Grand Port Battle, portraits of maritime personalities, wooden palanquins used by slaves to transport their masters, and artefacts recovered from East India Company shipwrecks. The most prized exhibits are the bell from the doomed *St Geran*, sunk off the east coast in 1744, and Labourdonnais' four-poster bed.

North of Mahebourg at Anse Jonchée is **Domaine du Chasseur** (open daily 9am–5pm; admission fee). A 1970s pioneer of eco-tourism, this former hunting estate has expanded into a popular 160-hectare (400-acre) reserve with steep walking trails through forests of spice plants and native trees. Mauritius kestrel, wild boar and deer are among the animal species found here. The restaurant has panoramic views of the reefs and islets of Vieux Grand Port. At **Domaine de Ylang Ylang** (open daily 9am–4pm; free), in the foothills of the same estate, an old distillery produces aromatic essential oil from locally grown ylang ylang plants, which you can buy in the adjacent shop.

Southwest of Mahebourg is the nature reserve of **Île aux Aigrettes** (open daily 9am–5pm; tel: 631 2396; admission fee), opposite the

**Domaine du Chasseur**

Preskil Beach Resort. The Mauritian Wildlife Foundation (MWF) created the reserve to protect native flora and fauna, so a trip here will appeal to the conservation-conscious rather than those wanting a water-based fun day out. Be advised that the island gets very hot (take a hat and water) and can accommodate only 20 visitors at a time on tours, which are led by knowledgeable MWF guides. You will see giant Aldabra tortoises and bands of the once-endangered pink pigeon, rare plants and paths bounded by bronze models of extinct fauna. During World War II the island was used for military purposes. The old generator room from that time has been renovated and includes a rooftop platform, which affords sweeping views of a canopy of indigenous trees that represent a microcosm of Mauritius's original coastal habitat. A shop and small museum display models and paintings of many extinct species.

Back on the mainland via the high-walled seaside bungalows of Pointe d'Esny the road ends at **Blue Bay**, where an idyllic beach backed by casuarina trees faces the private islet of Île des Deux Cocos. The area lies in a designated marine park, whose crystal-clear waters make for excellent snorkelling and diving.

## THE SOUTH

The remote, wild south, with its undulating cane-clothed landscapes, forests, waterfalls, rivers and mountains, has none of the bustle of the more popular tourist resorts of the north. Its appeal lies in its natural beauty and a feeling that you are going back in time. However, the west part of the south coast has undergone a transformation with the completion of smooth, wide roads that give access to hotels and inland attractions.

The southern beaches are narrower than elsewhere and rivers flowing from the uplands have prevented coral reefs from forming in many places. In the southwest corner of

**Panorama over Black River Gorges**

the island are the last of Mauritius's indigenous forests. By contrast, the southeast is a flatter, sugar-producing region of small towns and villages linked by roads crossing streams and rivers.

Whether you drive yourself or join a guided tour there are several ways of exploring the south: from Curepipe in the centre of the island, combining it with a trip to the Black River Gorges; from Bel Ombre in the west where a trio of luxurious hotels herald the start of an easy route east along the south coast; or from Mahebourg in the southeast.

## Black River Gorges National Park

Runaway slaves or *marrons* used to hide in the rugged mountains, gorges and forests that today make up the **Black River Gorges National Park**, an area of 6,575 hectares (16,250 acres) in the southwest. Elsewhere, little remains of the island's indigenous flora and fauna, but here you might

At the annual Maha Shivaratree festival at Grand Bassin, thousands of devotees make offerings to the goddess Shiva and pray at the waterside Hindu temples. At other times the lake is a place of quiet meditation broken only by the sound of birdsong and cheeky chattering monkeys.

spot the Mauritius kestrel and the green echo parakeet – two birds recently brought back from the brink of extinction – the white tropic bird, the cuckoo shrike and bands of macaque monkeys.

Many tourists combine a shopping trip to Curepipe *(see page 67)* with a scenic drive through the national park, heading southwest to La Marie and passing cool pine forests to the island's largest reservoir, **Mare aux Vacoas**. Continue for 7km (4 miles) to the crossroads called **Le Petrin**, where an information centre marks the entrance to the park. Here you can buy a map of the walking trails, or have a picnic in the adjacent Le Petrin Native Garden. The boardwalk leading over marshy heathland, where native flora and medicinal plants are being regenerated, is currently out of bounds.

A diversion 2km (1 mile) east of Le Petrin on the B88 takes you to the water-filled volcanic crater of **Grand Bassin** where a towering sculpture of the Hindu god Shri Mangal Mahadev was erected in 2006. It is the island's tallest statue at 32m (108ft). Hindus call the lake Ganga Talao ('Ganges Lake') as they believe that the waters are linked to the River Ganges in India.

Heading into the national park itself, drive south of Le Petrin via **Plaine Champagne**, an isolated plateau of privet choked with the invasive Chinese guava, whose fruit islanders gather for its vitamin C content in winter. On the way, keep an eye out for the *bois de pomme* and *bois de natte* trees, often draped with orchids, ferns and lichens, so characteristic of the island's upland forest. Further west are two viewpoints over the Black River Gorges. The first is **Alexandra Falls**, but the more spectacular views are from the **Black River Gorges Viewpoint**, 8km (5½ miles) from Le Petrin, where the deep, dark gorges unfold. The peaks of Rempart Mountain and Corps de Garde form a backdrop in the northwest.

The road twists and turns steeply downhill to **Chamarel** where coffee is grown on the slopes. This tiny village, with its church, village hall and string of simple restaurants, attracts tour groups heading to the **Waterfalls**, the highest in Mauritius at 83m (272ft). Best seen after heavy rains, the falls tumble from the River St Denis in the Black River Mountains to form the River du Cap.

**Chamarel Waterfalls**

Nearby are the **Coloured Earths**, a unique landscape of multi-coloured earth, thought to have been the result of uneven cooling of lava. Facilities include a cafeteria, shop, playground, and viewing platforms.

A tortuous but picturesque route from the Coloured Earths to Baie du Cap on the south coast cuts through sugar-cane fields and thick plantations of banana and travellers palms. At Baie du Cap turn left to join the B9 to Bel Ombre or right to reach Le Morne.

## Bel Ombre to Souillac

The area of **Bel Ombre** is associated with philanthropist and planter Charles Telfair, who arrived in Mauritius from Ireland in 1816. He bought the Bel Ombre Sugar Factory and turned it into a 'model sugar estate' by treating his slaves humanely, upsetting the local slave-owning fraternity by doing so. In 2004 the factory and banana plantations fringing the coast were cleared to make way for three hotels. Sugar is still grown in the area and transported to nearby factories, but all that remains of Telfair's factory are the chimney and outbuildings, which may one day become a museum.

Now occupying the site are the Telfair Hotel, an 18-hole golf course, and the elegant 19th-century **Chateau de Bel Ombre**, a former haven for visiting estate dignitaries that has been transformed into an upmarket restaurant. The Telfair, the Heritage and other neighbouring hotels can arrange excursions into the nearby private **Bel Ombre Nature Reserve**, where there are great walking trails, and horse-riding, quad- and mountain-biking opportunities. Steep, winding tracks lead to **Frederica**, where a ruined mill stands on the site of an old sugar factory. Further inland, **Val Riche Forest**, with its deer-hunting area and miradors, is home to many indigenous trees.

West of Bel Ombre is the small fishing village of **Baie du Cap**, followed by the magical deep inlet of the same name. Chug along the old concrete parapet across the bay, the Savanne Mountains forming a natural backdrop; this area will soon be given over to tourism development.

If you continue along the coast road, you reach Mauritius's most famous landmark and a symbol of slavery, **Le Morne Brabant**. This forebidding mountain towering over the hammerhead-shaped peninsula, now fringed with beach hotels, marks the former hideout of many runaway slaves. When slavery was abolished in 1835, a posse was sent here to

**Le Morne Brabant**

announce the news. Fearing that they would be hunted down, the runaway slaves flung themselves into the waters below rather than surrender.

East of Bel Ombre, the coast road speeds past cane fields, crossing bridges over the jungley banks of the **River Jacotet**. The river flows into **Jacotet Bay** opposite Ilot Sancho, where British and French troops clashed in 1810. There are rumours of buried pirates' treasure here.

The smooth B9 coast road from **Pointe aux Roches** to Riambel provides access to several hotels (currently under construction) and public beaches. Your hotel can organise a visit to the 2,400-hectare (6,000-acre) **St Felix Sugar Estate** at **Chamouny**, which includes a mountain lodge, spice garden, nature trail and restaurant. You can also drive inland from Chamouny to **Bassin Blanc**, where a precarious parking area allows views into a water-filled crater where the rare green echo parakeet and the Mauritius kestrel thrive in the

**Boats at Souillac**

surrounding forest. Further east, the sea off Pomponette is known for its treacherous currents, but there is safe swimming at SSR Public Beach just before the peaceful hamlet of Riambel.

There's nothing to detain you at Surinam, but it's worth stopping at **Souillac**, 2km (1 mile) further east, to explore a handful of nearby attractions. In the 19th century, steam ships laden with cane from nearby estates would shunt along the coast to Port Louis from the **old port**, on the banks of the River Savanne where a 200-year-old sugar warehouse has been converted into Le Batelage restaurant.

Just 5km (3 miles) inland from the old port, a bumpy ride through cane fields leads past the chimney of an early 19th-century sugar factory and the colourful Mariamen Temple before reaching the 10-m (33-ft) high **Rochester Falls**. The waters spill over from the Savanne River and years of erosion have shaped the basalt rock into upright columns. After heavy rains, young islanders use this place as an outdoor pool.

Just opposite Souillac's bus station is **Telfair Gardens**, perched on the edge of a cliff and shaded by Indian almond trees and banyans. To the west is the **Marine Cemetery**, which contains some of the island's oldest tombs, including those of Mauritian historian Baron d'Unienville (1766–1831) and poet and writer Robert Edward Hart (1891–1954), who lived in the village.

A 10-minute stroll east of Telfair Gardens is the **Robert Edward Hart Museum** (open daily 9am–4pm, Sat–Sun 9am–noon; free), Hart's former home. This prolific Franco-

Irish poet wrote works in French and English from this charming coral-built bungalow, which he called **Le Nef** (The Nave). The interior contains personal belongings, laid out much as he would have left them.

For views of a savagely wild coast from a grassy wind-swept headland, walk a few minutes east to **Le Gris Gris**, ◀ the most southerly point of Mauritius and a place rumoured to be associated with black magic. Some fine cliff walks reveal ghostly silhouettes of black rocks bashed by ferocious seas, including La Roche qui Pleure (The Crying Rock), which bears an uncanny resemblance to Hart's profile.

On the A9, 5km (3 miles) northeast of Souillac, is the grand 19th-century colonial residence of **St Aubin** (open ◀ daily 10am–3pm; free), set in spacious flower-bordered lawns dotted with trees and with an anthurium plantation.

## Colonial Homes

St Aubin is a fine example of a once widespread style of colonial architecture. Traditionally constructed from wood, colonial houses were kept cool by spacious and airy verandas at the front and rear, and by windows decorated with ornate wooden friezes or lambrequins. Wooden shutters could be closed during cyclone periods.

Unless maintained against the ravages of tropical conditions, wooden houses deteriorate very quickly and, sadly, many colonial houses have been allowed to fall into ruin. However, there are some superb privately owned residences hidden in the sugar estates and also in the back streets of Port Louis. The finest example is Eureka at Montagne Orry, which is set in beautiful grounds (see page 33). Others are Chateau de Mon Plaisir at Sir Seewoosagur Ramgoolam Botanic Gardens, Pamplemousses, (see page 41), and, at Moka, Le Réduit, the Mauritian president's official residence, which is open to the public twice a year (see page 65).

You can have tea on the veranda if the place isn't heaving with tour groups, or order lunch (reservations essential; tel: 626 1513). Tea is grown in the highlands around Bois Cheri 10km (6 miles) north. You can see how tea is processed and packaged at the **Bois Cheri Tea Museum and Factory** (open Mon–Sat 10am–4pm; free). A guided Tea Route Tour, which can be booked through tour operators, starts at Domaine des Aubineaux, a former tea planter's residence at Curepipe, and is followed by a visit to the factory, tea tasting at a hilltop pavilion and lunch at St Aubin.

At **Rivière des Anguilles**, also off the A9 and just after the river of the same name, is **La Vanille Reserve de Mascareigne** (open daily 9.30am–5pm; admission fee). Allow a couple of hours to visit this nature reserve, and douse yourself with insect repellent before exploring the shaded walking trails. You'll see thousands of commercially farmed Nile

**Giant tortoise and friend in La Vanille Reserve de Mascareigne**

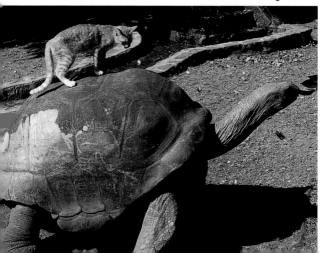

crocodiles in secure enclosures, luminous green geckos, chameleons, insects, butterflies and giant tortoises. A shop sells crocodile products and the restaurant specialises in crocodile meat dishes. Further north is the **Britannia Sugar Factory**, surrounded by spacious lawns and pineapple plantations. It is one of the last estates in the south that is still actively engaged in sugar production.

There's not much of interest on the B8, which heads east towards the airport at Plaine Magnien, other than a diversion to Le Souffleur, a blow hole in the cliff at L'Escalier midway along the coast. At one time during high tide, powerful waves would send spouts of water into the air. After years of erosion, the spout these days is more a cloud of spray.

## THE WEST

The island's 50-km (30-mile) long west coast, rapidly rising in popularity among overseas visitors, is dominated by the mountains and forests of the Black River area and fringed by white beaches and turquoise lagoons. The climate is hotter and drier than that of other parts of Mauritius. The seas off the Black River coast are a mecca for big-game fishermen, especially between September and March when warm waters attract giant marlin and tuna. Added to these attractions are fantastic sunsets, great inland nature walks, fabulous dive spots and easy access to Port Louis.

### South from Port Louis

Just off the A3 south from Port Louis and almost mid-way down the west coast is the popular resort of **Flic en Flac**. The concentration of restaurants, shops, supermarkets and Mediterranean-style apartment complexes can make it feel like a Creole version of the Costa del Sol, but the saving grace is the long white beach backed by casuarinas, a gentle lagoon and distant views of Le Morne Brabant in the south.

**Zebras in the Casela Nature and Leisure Park**

By contrast, **Wolmar**, less than 2km (1 mile) to the south, is quieter and dominated by half a dozen stylish beach-fronted hotels. All along the coast the diving is excellent, with a number of wrecks to explore, including *Kei Sei 113* and *Tug 11*, sunk deliberately in the 1980s to form artificial reefs *(see page 83)*.

The area north of the A3 cuts through the sugar-cane plantations of **Medine Sugar Estate**, which owns much of the land around Wolmar as well as the residential area of Albion. It is also one of the most successfully diversified estates on the west coast, with interests in tourism, golf resorts and real estate. During the cane-cutting season, tour operators may organise a guided tour of the factory, which also includes a distillery where you can buy local rum.

A few kilometres beyond the entrance to the sugar estate is the busy little village of **Bambous**. Tucked into cane fields to the north is **St Martin's Cemetery**, where you can see the graves of Jewish detainees who died in captivity at nearby Beau Bassin Prison during World War II *(see page 59)*.

► **Casela Nature and Leisure Park** (open daily 9am–5pm; admission fee), on the A3 south from Bambous, makes a break from the beach and a fun day out. You could easily spend a whole day at the 10-hectare (25-acre) park, which sits on the flanks of Rempart Mountain. As well as some 1,500 birds, including the rare Mauritius kestrel and pink pigeon, housed in 90 aviaries, there are giant Aldabra tortoises, tigers, lemurs, antelopes and zebras. Children can touch some of the animals in a petting area and from the restaurant there are panoramic views of rolling cane-clothed countryside. The more adventurous can join photo safaris, go rock climbing, quad- and mountain-biking or join exciting nature escapades crossing rivers and streams in the adjacent Yemen Estate, where Java deer roam in a savannah landscape reminiscent of Africa. You are very likely to spot wild boar, hare, giant fruit bats and mongoose.

## Tamarin

**Tamarin**, 6km (4 miles) south, famous for its salt-making industry, is named after the tamarind trees, introduced by the Dutch, that are a feature of the area, especially in the undulating terrain of the Tamarina Golf Estate. Luxury villas and an 18-hole golf course make Tamarin a fashionable place to holiday. The stylish **Riverland Sports and Leisure Complex**, with a large pool and cafeteria, attracts a trendy, fun crowd; the refurbished Tamarin Hotel stages regular jazz nights, and the bay attracts dolphins and body

### Jewish Detainees

In the grey-walled St Martin's Cemetery, 127 identical tombstones are a reminder of events that took place during World War II. In 1940, British authorities refused 1,580 Eastern European Jewish refugees entry to Palestine. Regarded as 'illegal immigrants', they were shipped to Mauritius and detained in refugee camps at Beau Bassin Prison. They remained there until the end of the war. Families still return to Mauritius to visit the graves of those who died in the camps.

surfers. Meanwhile, the village retains a timeless atmosphere, its seaside bungalows and cheap pensions fringing a tranquil bay where the coral reef is subdued by waters flowing from the Rempart and Tamarin rivers in the central highlands. At sunset there are magnificent views of Rempart Mountain, looking for all the world like a mini-Matterhorn in a tropical setting.

The **Martello Tower Museum** (open Tues–Sat 9.30am–5pm, Sun 9.30am–1.30pm; admission fee), at **La Preneuse**, sits on the northern side of the Grande Rivière Noire Bay, 2km (1 mile) south of Tamarin. It is the best-preserved Martello tower in Mauritius and has walls that are 3.5m (11ft) thick. A visit takes you past cannon and the paraphernalia needed to fire them, including cannon balls; you'll see the fascinating engineering of the tower, how rain was collected in underground reservoirs and how gunpowder was kept dry. The British built this and four other towers on the large bays of the west coast to protect against enemy invasion at a time when there was much rivalry between the French-speaking population and the British authorities over the intended emancipation of slaves. Two other towers survive – at La Harmonie, to the south of the Grande Rivière Noire Bay, and at Pointe aux Sables, just outside Port Louis.

> **Martello towers were defensive forts built by the British in various coastal locations in Britain and the empire during the Napoleonic Wars. Their round shape and thick walls gave them great resistance to cannon fire.**

Still on the A3 south, the next village, **Grand Rivière Noire**, is the west coast's game-fishing centre *(see page 81)*. Off the coast, and beyond the reef, the seabed drops abruptly to a depth of nearly 600m (2,000ft), the habitat of several big-game species. Just before the village, opposite the

**Grand Rivière Noire**

Pavillion de Jade restaurant, a road cuts through sugar cane for 5km (3 miles) to the northern entrance of the Black River Gorges National Park *(see page 49)*. You can only drive as far as the visitors centre (open daily 9am–5pm), where you can collect maps and information. Serious hikers may enjoy an uphill 10-km (6-mile) trek along the strenuous Macchabée Trail, crossing rivers and streams, to a spectacular forest viewpoint. The other way to get into the park by car is to drive south to **Grande Case Noyale** and turn inland to Chamarel *(see page 51)*.

Grand Rivière Noire village sits on the estuary of a river that flows through some of the most rugged areas on the island. Once the poorest region of Mauritius, with a predominantly Afro-Creole population, the area is showing signs of prosperity, although life still trundles on at a leisurely pace. A gated complex of posh hillside villas and the gleaming shopping and restaurant complex of Ruisseau Creole contrast sharply with the brightly painted stores, simple eateries and weathered timber-built colonial **post office** and **police station** of the village further on. Next to the post office is the **cemetery**, where the founder of the Mauritius Turf Club, Colonel Edward Draper, is buried.

At **Grande Case Noyale**, the cream-coloured church of Mater Dolorosa lies at the foot of a steep road marking the turn-off for the 5-km (3-mile) drive to Chamarel. The road was originally built in 1812 to give access to the remote uplands and, although it is well surfaced, there are numerous hairpin bends. Spectacular views of the west coast unfold as you climb the timbered foothills of the Black River Mountains, and you may spot bands of macaque monkeys on the way. Two restaurants, La Crete and Varangue-sur-Morne, perched in the hills, provide panoramic views of the countryside, coast and clam-shaped **Île aux Benitiers** nestling in the lagoon. Both establishments are good pit stops before pressing on for the Coloured Earths and Waterfalls *(see page 51)*.

## THE PLATEAU TOWNS

The towns of the plateau have merged into one unattractive urban sprawl to form the district of Plaine Wilhems in the centre of the island. Some 30 percent of the island's population live in this busy, boisterous and often traffic-choked region. In spite of these negatives, the towns are worth visiting for an insight into local lifestyles, and the shopping is fun, the climate is cooler than elsewhere and there are isolated pockets of architectural interest.

The towns were formed a little more than 100 years ago as a result of several migrations from Port Louis after fire, disease and cyclones sent inhabitants scurrying to the healthier uplands. Today the area of Plaine Wilhems contains the towns of Rose Hill–Beau Bassin, Quatre Bornes, Vacoas–Phoenix and Curepipe.

Many tour operators offer shopping trips to the towns, often combining them with a drive into the Black River Gorges *(see page 49)*, but you can just as easily drive yourself by taking the marked exits anywhere along the motorway which links Mahebourg in the south with Grand Baie in the north.

## Rose Hill–Beau Bassin

The Royal Road links the towns of **Rose Hill** and **Beau Bassin**, which are effectively one, with a combined population of 90,000. Rose Hill's centrepiece is the Victorian-built **post office**, a former railway station, standing proud amid the chaos of the bus station fringed by ubiquitous food stalls and shopping arcades. The town is showing signs of modernity, new roads leading east past weather-beaten buildings to the Cyber City complex at Ebene. Here, **Cyber Tower I**,

**The Plaza Theatre, part of the Town Hall in Rose Hill–Beau Bassin**

(Cyber Tower II is under construction), a seven-storey symbol of 21st-century development, reflects the island's desire to become a leader of information technology in the Indian Ocean region.

Meanwhile **Arab Town**, in Royal Road, Rose Hill's main shopping street, is a reminder of the immediate present. Here, you can barter for just about anything under the sun among an untidy collection of corrugated-iron covered stalls. Nearby, tumbledown shops are packed with incongruous displays of everything from statues of Hindu gods and the Virgin Mary to cosmetics and car parts. Further south is the colonial-style **Town Hall**, dating back to 1927 and a fine example of Creole architecture, and the Max Boullé Art Gallery, which sometimes exhibits works by local artists.

**Beau Bassin**, north along the Royal Road, is less frenetic than Rose Hill and has a couple of sights worth visiting. **Balfour Gardens** (open daily 6am–6pm) in Swami Sivananda Street, has great views of the Moka Mountains across a ravine to a waterfall, which tumbles into the Grande Rivière North West. Next door is **Le Thabor**, a

## Invitation to a Ball

Le Réduit was the setting for a piece of philatelic history in 1847. In that year, the Mauritian colonial authorities introduced postage stamps, one with a value of one penny, the other of two pennies. Britain had issued the first stamp only seven years before. The story goes that a local engraver was told to produce the stamps quickly so that some of them could be used by the governor's wife, Lady Gomm, to send invitations to a ball at the residence. The stamps, bearing the head of Queen Victoria, were mistakenly printed with 'Post Office' instead of 'Post Paid'. The mistake has made the few surviving examples very highly valued by collectors.

**Sugar-cane fields and the Moka Mountains**

Catholic church pastoral centre. Charles Darwin stayed here in 1836, leading him to remark, 'How pleasant it would be to pass one's life in such quiet abodes'. More ravine views unfold in this tranquil area, dubbed 'The English Quarter' during colonial times when British diplomats and the aristocracy lived here.

At **Moka**, 4km (2 miles) east of Rose Hill, is the modern university complex and **Le Réduit**, the president's official residence (open twice a year; check with the tourist office for dates). The French built this magnificent chateau in 1748 on a peninsula isolated by two ravines as a country residence and retreat for the wives and children of the French East India Company in the event of an invasion. It later became the British governor's residence. Nearby, the Mahatma Gandhi Institute has the **Folk Museum of Indian Immigration** (open Mon–Fri 9am–3.30pm; free), which traces the 19th-century migration of Indian cane workers to Mauritius.

Hindu temple on Corps de Garde Mountain

## Quatre Bornes

Many people speed through **Quatre Bornes** after a shopping trip to the modern shopping mall at **Trianon**, unaware that there are some lovely colonial houses tucked away in the back streets. *La Foire* market, on Wednesday and Saturday in the heart of town, has good buys in clothing, textiles, household goods, and fruit and vegetables, and there are reasonable shops and eateries in the main Grand Route St Jean. To the west is the distinctive **Corps de Garde Mountain** at 720m (2,326ft), which runaway slaves used as a lookout post. Rising up the flanks of the mountain are Hindu temples where Tamil devotees celebrate the annual Cavadee Festival *(see page 94)*. To the south is the hump-shaped **Candos Hill**.

## Vacoas–Phoenix

**Vacoas** was a former British land-based communications base, HMS *Mauritius*, whose old colonial-style buildings are now the headquarters of the paramilitary Special Mobile Force. The chaos of the bus station and market, so character-istic of many Mauritian towns, is mitigated by more tranquil scenes: glimpses of rural England, with quiet, shaded av-enues, an 18-hole golf course at the private Gymkhana Club and the stone-built **St Columba's Church**, where services are held monthly in English.

**Phoenix** is home to a brewery producing the local beer, as well as food-manufacturing companies and the sprawling Jumbo shopping complex. Nearby, the **Mauritius Glass Gallery** (open Mon–Sat 9am–5pm; free) includes a small museum featuring exhibits by various conservation groups, such as the Mauritian Wildlife Foundation and Friends of the Environment. In the workshop you can watch glass-blowers, who use recycled glass, and buy unusual products in the adjacent showroom.

## Curepipe

**Curepipe**, the highest plateau town at 550m (1,840ft), is sit-uated halfway between Mahebourg and Port Louis. In the 18th century, soldiers and travellers would rest and 'cure' or clean their pipes, hence the name. It was the first plateau town to be settled, mainly by the Franco-Mauritian popula-tion in the 1860s, who spilled into the suburbs of **Floreal** and **Forest Side**, where their descendants still live in grand colo-nial houses hidden by high bamboo hedges.

Invariably cloud-capped and rainy, the town is not partic-ularly inspiring, but a shopping expedition can turn up some good buys: porcelain and silk in the Chinese shops in Royal Road; stunning fabrics, *objets d'art*, Oriental carpets and fashion accessories at Etoile d'Orient in John Kennedy Street; and sophisticated knitwear at Floreal, where the modern **Textile Museum** (open Mon–Fri 9am–5pm, Sat 9.30am–1pm; free) traces the development of the textile

> To the west of Curepipe are the 2-hectare (5-acre) Botanical Gardens in Botanical Gardens Street. Its avenues, bounded by lakes, lawns and indigenous plants, are perfect for a quiet stroll.

industry with the aid of interactive displays and a short film. At Forest Side, next door to the **Comajora Model Boat Factory** in La Brasserie Road, is the privately run **Boat Museum** ◀ (open Mon–Fri 8am–5pm; free). It's worth visiting for its collection of over 100 model boats. The museum's owner is passionate about sailing history and is happy to share his knowledge with visitors. Curepipe is also a popular gateway to the Black River Gorges *(see page 49)*.

Curepipe's most attractive buildings are sandwiched between Elizabeth Avenue and Ste Theresa Street near the market, whose concrete chimneys rise like foghorns against an often grey sky. Here the 1920s-built **Carnegie Library** and the impressive Creole-style architecture of the **Town Hall** contrast with the modern Lake Point complex, with its shops, ice-skating rink and casino. The complex overlooks gardens containing a bronze statue of Paul and Virginie, star-crossed lovers of the *St Geran* shipwreck *(see page 40)* and the central characters in Bernadin de St Pierre's romantic 18th-century novel.

Also worth visiting is **Trou aux Cerfs**, a 15-minute walk or short taxi ride (vehicular access between 8am and 4pm) from the centre of town. This 300-m (980-ft) diameter crater was formed as a result of volcanic activity millions of years ago and is now choked with silt, water and a dense forest of vegetation. At 650m (2,100ft) above sea level you could be on the roof of paradise were it not for the urban sprawl of the plateau towns below, but the views of the mountains, especially on a clear day, are truly spectacular.

# RODRIGUES

The island of Rodrigues, a semi-autonomous region of Mauritius since 2002, lies 560km (350 miles) east of Mauritius. Shaped like a fish, it is 18km (11 miles) long and 8km (5 miles) wide, making it the smallest of the Mascarene trio. Only a few navigable channels penetrate the fringing coral reef, which protects a lagoon almost twice the island's size. Running the length of Rodrigues is a hilly ridge, from which a series of steep valleys drop to a narrow coastline. Even though the flight from Mauritius takes only 90 minutes, you can't help feeling quarantined from the rest of the world when you bump along the runway at Plaine Corail airport in the south. If you have time, you can go to Rodrigues by ship *(see page 115)*.

About 37,000 people live here. The island's distinct Creole-African atmosphere is in complete contrast to Indian-

**Collecting firewood, Rodrigues**

dominated Mauritius. Also unlike Mauritius, the island is a relative newcomer to tourism. With stunning coves and bays, deserted beaches, a shallow islet-dotted lagoon, great diving, snorkelling, hilly walking trails, duty-free shopping, and a friendly, courteous people, Rodrigues makes a simple, unpretentious and at times quirky holiday destination.

## Port Mathurin

**Port Mathurin**, the pint-sized capital, is home to 5,390 people. It sits snugly on the north coast and was probably named after a French settler, Mathurin Morlaix, who arrived in 1726. Under the French, slaves from Mozambique and Madagascar, and settlers from Mauritius, increased the population to just over 100 in 1804. Nobody took much notice of Rodrigues until the British launched an attack from its shores before taking Mauritius in 1810. They restructured Port Mathurin and laid out the present town in grid style, naming many streets after surveyors and civil servants, which islanders still refer to, in spite of being officially renamed by the regional authority.

### François Leguat

François Leguat led the first group of settlers on Rodrigues in 1691, and left behind a fascinating record of his time there, *Voyages and Adventures*. In it, he describes the island's unique flora and fauna, the latter including a species of giant tortoise weighing over 135kg (300lb). There were so many tortoises that the beaches were covered in them, and Leguat used the shells as stepping stones to reach the sea (the species later became extinct). The book was so accurate that 19th-century naturalists and geologists used it as an early textbook. Today, all that is left to remember Leguat is an unimaginative riverside monument and a commemorative postage stamp.

**Selling chutneys and chillies in Port Mathurin market**

A good place to start your exploration is from the boat-shaped jetty on the waterfront where a **memorial** stands to volunteers who fought in World Wars I and II.

The Saturday **market** in Fishermen Lane attracts early risers as islanders set up stalls of fruit and vegetables at 6am. You can find souvenirs like baskets and wallets made from woven vacoas leaves, as well as bottles of chillies, home-made chutneys, and fruit and vegetables. The market sells out quickly, and by 10am everybody has packed up and gone home.

The main artery of the town is **Jenner Street**, one block back from the waterfront, where shops, no more than corrugated iron shacks with handwritten nameplates nailed to the door, contrast with a rash of duty-free shops in Duncan and Morrison streets. In Douglas Street you can find unusual handicrafts, such as snazzy briefcases, straw hats and fiery home-bottled chillies. At the western end of Jenner Street is the tiny, white six-minareted **Noor-ud-Deen Mosque**. The island's only mosque, it was built in 1912 for the first Muslim settlers, who had arrived in 1907 as textile merchants.

Still in Jenner Street, hidden by white walls and fronted by a cannon, is the last vestige of British colonialism, the 1873 **Island Secretary's Residence**, now used for official receptions. It's not open to the public, but you can peep through the gates and see the wide veranda shaded by a gnarled Indian almond tree beneath which visiting colonial experts once discussed the next big move in island affairs.

A short stroll east leads to the Anglican **St Barnabas Church**, shaded by gardens and trees. Originally designed by an Eastern Telegraph cableman in 1903 as a shingle-roofed wooden chapel, it's been modernised and enlarged to encompass the Rodrigues College. Most Rodriguans are Catholics and the little **Saint Coeur de Marie Church** in Ricard Street sees a regular Sunday congregation. The daubing of foreheads with ashes in the sign of the cross on Ash Wednesday, and processions on Easter Day, are serious traditions.

Over the **Winston Churchill Bridge**, which crosses the River Cascade, is the location of the first settlement on the island, in 1691, by French Huguenots fleeing religious persecution. Led by François Leguat *(see page 70)*, they lived for the next two years on 'very wholesome and luxurious foods which never caused the least sickness', as Leguat wrote, and feasted on fruit and palm wine, before returning to Mauritius only to be imprisoned by the Dutch on Île aux Phares as spies.

Further upriver towards **Fond La Digue** is Port

> **Next to the Careco Workshop is the Gonzague Pierre-Louis Special Learning Centre (Mon–Fri 8am–2pm), a school for sight- and hearing-impaired children. Pupils are genuinely pleased to receive visitors and the teachers are happy to give you a tour.**

Mathurin's only hotel, the delightful Creole-style Escale Vacances, set in a wooded valley overlooking the river. You can have some adventurous uphill walks along a jungley boulder-strewn track to Mont Lubin, where at dusk the Rodrigues fruit bat comes out to feed on jamrosa trees.

For unique island handicrafts, visit the **Careco Workshop** (open Mon–Fri 8am–3pm, Sat 8am–noon) at Camp du Roi at the back of town, where items are made by disabled people. An apiary also produces the clear and distinctly flavoured Rodriguan honey, which has consistently won international awards. Visitors wanting some nightlife, meanwhile, should look out for hand-written bills advertising *une grande soiree dansante*. These are big nights out, not to be missed, when you can let your hair down. On pay days and holidays or roughly once a month, everyone from babes in arms to robust Rodriguan grannies bop to seggae and reggae beneath flashing lights, and smooching couples cling to each other like clams. Try the alfresco discos at Les Cocotiers at Camp du Roi or the Recif at Anse aux Anglais.

**View over Port Mathurin**

## Around Port Mathurin

A short stroll to the east of Port Mathurin is **Anse aux Anglais** (English Bay) where in 1761 a British fleet arrived and stayed for six months. Like the French ships that came before them, the Royal Navy's vessels transported thousands of giant tortoises – valued for their meat – from here to neighbouring Réunion. By the end of the 18th century, the Rodrigues tortoise, which originally may have numbered around 200,000, had become extinct.

In 1901 cablemen from the Eastern Telegraph Company (later Cable & Wireless) laid a submarine telegraph cable linking the island with Mauritius, thus completing the line of communication between Australia and Europe. The cablemen lived in quarters at nearby **Pointe Venus** where

**Octopus drying, Anse aux Anglais**

the manager's colonial-style residence, which later saw service as the island's first hotel, has re-opened as a completely rebuilt three-star billet. There are good views across Port Mathurin from the headland where French and British astronomers recorded the transit of Venus in 1761 and then again in 1874.

At low tide, near the Pointe Venus Hotel, groups of fisherwomen, known as *piqueuses ourites*, make their living spearing octopus, which they hang out to dry in the sun. A stiff uphill climb from Anse aux Anglais via the tranquil beach-side bungalows of **Caverne Provert** leads to a headland where there are resplendent views over sandy-bottomed **Grand Baie**, just 4km (2 miles) east of Port Mathurin. It's a lovely spot with only a church and makeshift football pitch (the latter patronised by Prince William when he visited in 2003). From Grand Baie the road peters out to become a narrow uphill track that leads towards the sweeping deserted beach at **Baladirou**. A less strenuous way of getting there is to take a 40-minute boat ride along the coast from Port Mathurin.

Just 2km (1 mile) to the west of Port Mathurin is **Baie aux Huitres** (Oyster Bay), an enormous bay surrounded by hills and deep forests of casuarinas. Many civil servants posted from Mauritius live here with their families, along with the predominantly European descendants of the first French settlers. For the best views, drive up to **Allée Tamarin**, a hamlet at the back of the bay.

## Inland from Port Mathurin

The bus station to the west of Port Mathurin has plenty of buses to take you on a bone-shaking journey around fearsome hairpin bends to the spine of the island, where little villages overlook the north and south lagoons. Buses stop at around 4pm, so leave plenty of time to return.

At **Pointe Canon** there are panoramic views of the capital. On this windswept headland you'll find a British cannon juxtaposed with a white statue of the Virgin Mary, **La Reine de Rodrigues**. On 1 May, the approach road and hills are a riot of colour with islanders trekking towards the statue to celebrate Labour Day. On 15 August, large numbers attend outdoor mass here to celebrate Assumption Day. The road climbs to **Solitude**, where a forest bounded by deep valleys and eucalyptus trees is the habitat of colonies of fruit bats.

**Mont Lubin**, a busy little village of tumbledown shops, gives the impression of being at the top of the island, but the highest point is **Mont Limon** at 393m (1,289ft), a five-minute walk east. Many tourists pass this way to visit **Grande Montagne Nature Reserve** (tel: 832 5737) for its walking trails and small museum, before continuing to Pointe Coton and the isolated eastern beaches.

Rodrigues' biggest place of worship, the twin-towered Gothic-style Cathedral of Sacre-Coeur, is west along the Mont Lubin road at **Saint Gabriel**. Islanders built the cathedral in 1939, using donkeys to carry sand from the coast, and their own labour to bring cement, lime, blocks of coral, corrugated iron and timber up the narrow mountain paths. It seats 2,000 people and Sunday morning mass is a colourful event.

The 5-km (3-mile) stretch of road between the hamlets of **Petit Gabriel**, **Quatre Vents** and **La Mangue** is peppered with glimpses of translucent blue lagoons bordered by a thin pencil-line of ivory-white foam marking the reef

You have to pass through **La Ferme**, a large noisy village, where Pope John Paul II held mass in 1989, to reach **Cascade Pistache**, 2km (1 mile) west of the village. This crater,

## Île Cocos

For a day that will stay in your memory long after the holiday snaps have been stashed away, don't miss Île Cocos, 4km (2 miles) west of Rodrigues. Here you'll have nothing to do but pad barefoot along floury white beaches beside a gin-clear lagoon while listening to the chatter of birds. This island, one of 18 inside Rodrigues lagoon, was transformed into a nature reserve in 1980 after studies revealed that out of an estimated 12 species of indigenous birds only two were left. It is now the last refuge of the fody and the brush warbler. Tour operators will arrange the necessary permits for a visit. The boat ride to Île Cocos ends 1km (½ mile) from shore because of shallow water; you walk the rest of the way.

**Cyclone-proof houses in the village of Songes**

hewn out of granite, is surrounded by grassy hills; the water-fall tumbling into Rivière Pistache is particularly beautiful after heavy rains. Alternatively, take the road northwards to **Baie du Nord** for a scenic 9-km (5-mile) coastal drive back to Port Mathurin, passing isolated homesteads swathed in poinsettias, hibiscus and marigolds, and causeways filled with mangroves at **Baie Malgache**.

## The South

From Mont Lubin, in the centre of the island, it is only a 6-km (3½-mile) journey to **Port Sud-Est**. The road snakes its way down hillsides, twisting and turning along a series of hairpin bends, each giving glorious vistas of Port Sud-Est, where small coral atolls dot the lagoon. Your journey's end is the **Morouk Hotel**, sitting in an isolated clifftop location. The nearest village is **Songes**, where boxy cyclone-proof houses are scattered on the hillsides like dominoes. Attractions

**Cotton Bay Hotel**

include leisurely walks to the pretty beach of **Petit Gravier** along the coast, and picnic and snorkelling excursions to Hermitage and Cat islands.

A visit to the coral caves in the southwest corner of the island at **Caverne Patate** should not be missed, although it is not for the faint-hearted or claustrophobic. These caves, some 18m (60ft) below the ground, have fascinated naturalists ever since the first official exploration in 1786 when bones, thought at the time to be those of the dodo, were found by a French captain. Later searches by British naturalists in 1894 led to more bone discoveries, and comparisons with earlier findings proved that they belonged to a relative of the dodo, the solitaire, which François Leguat had described in 1691.

Early accounts record that the caves contained 'superb petrifications of an infinite variety of shapes all different from each other'; today's guides insist that there are rock lookalikes of Winston Churchill and the Great Wall of China. Wear strong, sturdy shoes, bring a torch and don't lose sight of the guide as you stumble through pitch-dark passages studded with stalagmites and stalactites to emerge 550m (500yds) later on *terra firma*.

## The East

The **Cotton Bay Hotel**, at Pointe Coton in the east, was the first three-star hotel to open in Rodrigues and is popular with walkers and beach lovers. It is flanked by low coral cliffs and overlooks the best swimming beach of the island. From here you can walk to **Roche Bon Dieu**, a phallus-shaped rock symbol protruding from the earth and said to be a gift from God. There are more superb beaches, accessed by pathways on coral-topped cliffs, to **Anse Ally**, **Saint François** and **Baie de l'Est** and to the protected forest land at **Tasman**. Due east from here the nearest landfall is the western coast of Australia, some 5,500km (3,410 miles) away.

The forested area is fenced off to stop cattle grazing, but the watchman will let you in to experience some wonderful walks. Paths bounded by great forests of casuarina trees and acacias lead to a plateau of dead coral, where massive white rollers pound the reef, in some places less than 100m (300ft) from the shore. From here the paths rise and dip into the lovely coves and bays of **Grand Anse**, **Trou d'Argent** and **Anse Bouteille** before linking up to Port Sud-Est.

**The cove of Trou d'Argent**

## WHAT TO DO

### SPORTS

Mauritius' greatest attraction is, of course, the sea. The coastal waters, with few exceptions, offer safe swimming in shallow blue lagoons. Most hotels offer free water-based activities, which include snorkelling, windsurfing, water-skiing, sailing in hobie cats, use of pedalos, and trips in glass-bottom boats. Scuba diving, big-game fishing and parasailing are also popular and can be booked through hotels or independent tour operators. Similar facilities are available in Rodrigues, but since that island's lagoon is shallow there are no motorised water sports or parasailing and big-game fishing is relatively new.

The seabed and coral reefs are the habitat of myriad colourful fish and other marine creatures. Several operators offer enticing excursions, such as dolphin-watching cruises, underwater safaris, cruising to offshore islands and helicopter tours, which give magnificent views of the lagoons and coastline.

Recent years have seen a proliferation of green tourism ventures, for which reservations are essential. The undulating landscapes are ideal for horse-riding, quad-biking, four-wheel drive 'soft' safaris, mountain-biking, cycling and canyoning. Golfing on scenic courses, tennis, walking and hiking are also very popular.

### Water Activities

**Big-game fishing**. Mauritius holds the world record for big marlin and hosts the annual Marlin World Cup competition in November at the Centre de Pêche, Grand Rivière Noire, in the southwest. The best time for big-game fishing is between October and the end of March or April, when the waters beyond the reef teem with powerful blue and black marlin, yellow-fin tuna, wahoo, sailfish, bonito and various species of shark. The larger hotels have their own boats, and a number of private companies offer fishing excursions, such as the Corsaire Club (tel: 265 5209), the Hotel Club Centre de Pêche (tel: 683 6522) and Sportfisher (tel: 263 6309) at Grand Baie. A one-day fishing trip for a maximum of five people is R16,000 and includes lunch and drinks in a fully equipped boat with experienced crew. In Rodrigues contact BDPM Fishing (tel: 831 2790) or Sailfish (tel: 831 1623).

**Sailing**. Cruising in catamarans or yachts along the coast or to visit offshore islands is immensely popular. Many charter companies offer full- or half-day excursions that include lunch, drinks and snorkelling equipment. One of the best is Land and Sea Adventures (tel/fax: 261 1724) at Pointe aux Piments, which offers romantic sunset cruises and an exhilarating day out to Gabriel Island.

In Rodrigues you can sail to several deserted islands within the lagoon through Rodtours (tel: 831 2249).

For a trip back in time, try a cruise on the 150-year-old *Isla Mauritia*, which you can book through your hotel or direct through Yacht Charters (tel: 263 8395). This magnificent sailing ship, with a crew in turn-of-the-19th-century uniforms, sails from Grand Baie and drops anchor at Baie du Tombeau for a barbecue lunch and snorkelling.

**Scuba diving**. Dozens of dive centres, all affiliated to CMAS (World Underwater Federation), PADI (Professional Association of Diving Instructors) and BSAC (British Sub Aqua Club), are attached to hotels and offer courses for beginners and the more experienced. All adhere to strict international safety regulations and provide multi-lingual instructors, plus all the necessary equipment.

**Cruising with the 150-year-old *Isla Mauritia* (see box opposite)**

Beginners start off in the hotel pool before taking the plunge into the lagoon. Veteran divers should head for the long-established dive centre based at Villa Caroline at Flic en Flac, which offers specialist and night diving.

Some of the best dive sites are off the west coast at Flic en Flaq where there are several wrecks to explore, including the *Kei Sei 113* and *Tug 11*, sunk deliberately in the 1980s to form artificial reefs and now home to giant moray eels and myriad reef fish. Popular dives in the north include the wreck of *The Silver Star*, from 1992, and between two off-shore islands, Gabriel and Flat. In the east, the prevailing winds limit diving opportunities, but some interesting dives can be made in and around the passes through the reef. The best place to dive on the south coast is at the Blue Bay Marine Park where a sheltered lagoon and several sites beyond the reef will reward you with spectacular views of underwater life. On Rodrigues there are dive centres at the

**Excursion boat at Île aux Cerfs**

Cotton Bay Hotel (tel: 831 8001) and Mourouk Ebony Hotel (tel: 832 3350).

**Snorkelling**. Many visitors are content to spend their entire holiday snorkelling in the safety of the lagoon and over the shallow reefs. If you're staying in a hotel, all equipment is provided; if you're not, there's no shortage of shops selling masks, fins and goggles. You can also buy waterproof laminated cards from bookshops, which identify some 40 common species of reef fish. Even if spending a short time snorkelling, do wear a T-shirt and douse yourself in high-factor sun cream to avoid sunburn.

**Submarine safaris**. For an hour-long trip in a submarine that explores some interesting shipwrecks, contact Blue Safari Submarine (tel: 263 3333, <www.bluesaf.com>). *Le Nessee*, bookable through Croisieres Australes (tel: 674 3695) is a semi-submersible vessel with particularly good viewing chambers that enable you to have eyeball-to-eyeball contact with many marine species. Both the Blue Safari Submarine and *Le Nessee* leave from Grand Baie.

**Undersea walks**. A boat takes you from the shore to a platform inside the lagoon and, wearing your swimsuit, you are equipped with a helmet, which supplies fresh air piped from the surface by oil-free compressors. You are then gently lowered from the platform to the seabed where you can stroll amid wonderful coral gardens and even feed the fish by hand. The helmet allows verbal communication with an experienced diver, who gives you a guided tour of the lagoon. This activity is perfectly safe for children over seven, and will also appeal to non-swimmers. Undersea walks can be booked through your hotel or direct through Captain Nemo's Undersea Walks (tel: 263 7819, email: undersea@intnet.mu) at Grand Baie. This company offers similar facilities at Belle Mare.

## Land-based Activities

**Adventure Tourism**. Mauritius is just starting to tap its potential for adventurous activities. Extreme sports enthusiasts can go canyoning and rock-climbing with Vertical World (tel: 254 6607, www.verticalworldltd.com>), which also has great hiking opportunities. Casela Leisure and Nature Park (tel: 452 0693, <www.casela yemen.mu>) offers similar activities, as well as photo safaris. For quad- and mountain-biking and trail-walking contact: Domaine du Chasseur (tel: 634 5097, <www.domaineduchasseur.mu>); L'Etoile (tel: 433 1010, <www.cieletnature.com>); or Yemaya (tel: 752 0046,

**Rock-climbing at Casela**

<www.yemayaadventures.com>). Yemaya also offers sea kayaking and hiking. Espace Aventure (tel: 670 4301, <www.mttb-maurtourco.com>) has several four-wheel drive 'soft' safari options into the hinterland to see hidden landscapes and indigenous wildlife. In the Black River Gorges National Park (tel: 507 0128), starting from Le Petrin or from the Black River Visitors Centre in the lower gorges, there are some 60km (37 miles) of easy to strenuous walking trails through tropical and dwarf native forests. When choosing an operator for an adventurous activity, see the important health and medical-care information on *pages 116–17*, and check your travel insurance to make sure you're covered in case of accident.

**Horse-riding**. A number of stables take visitors on rides through breathtaking hills and countryside, including Vieille Cheminee (tel: 686 5027) at Chamarel, which has five gentle horses; Domaine les Pailles (tel 286 4225), just outside Port Louis; La Ranch (tel: 483 5478) at Black River; and Horse Riding Delights (tel: 265 6159) at Mon Choisy Leisure Park. Rides start from R1,550 per adult and R1,350 for children under the age of 15. The Maritim Hotel, on the northwest coast, also has private stables for the use of guests. Reservations for horse-riding are essential.

**An idyllic place for golf**

**Hunting**. Deer and wild-boar hunting are traditional Mauritian pastimes, and are becoming popular with some visitors. Contact Domaine du Chasseur (tel: 634 5097) to arrange a hunting party with overnight accommodation in rustic bungalows. The

**Horse-riding at Mon Choisy Leisure Park**

hunting season for deer is from June to September. Wild-boar hunting is a year-round activity.

**Cycling**. The flat coastal regions make for some easy rides. Bikes can be booked through your hotel, and there are plenty of operators in the resorts who rent bikes by the hour, half day or full day.

**Golf**. There are nine-hole courses at Trou aux Biches (tel: 204 6565), St Geran (tel: 415 1825), Shandrani (tel: 603 4343), Maritim (tel: 204 1000) and Sofitel (tel: 453 8700). There are 18-hole courses at Belle Mare Plage (tel: 415 1501), Tamarin (tel: 423 8595), Paradis (tel: 450 5050) and Heritage Hotel (tel: 601 1500), and at Île aux Cerfs (tel: 402 7400) on the east coast. Equipment, clubs and caddies can be hired. All hotels have a clubhouse with a locker room and shop. Pros can also be hired for lessons. Non-guests have to pay an entry fee. There is also a private 18-hole course at the Gymkhana Club at Vacoas.

Racing at Champs de Mars in Port Louis

## Other Activities

**Horse Racing**. Mauritians are passionate about horse racing. The season begins in May and culminates in November with the Maiden Cup, the grandest and most important race of the year. Races are held every Saturday afternoon and some Sundays at Champs de Mars in Port Louis. There is an entry fee, but if a member invites you, don't turn the chance down as you can have excellent views of the track from a private box or from the terrace. For further information contact the Mauritius Turf Club (tel: 212 2212, <www.mauritiusturfclub.com>).

**Helicopter Tours**. One of the best ways to take in the island's scenery is by air. Air Mauritius helicopters (tel: 603 3754) offer sightseeing tours and splendid photographic opportunities of the coast and interior. A 15-minute trip costs R18,000 per helicopter, which can seat four people.

**Spas**. The larger hotels have luxurious spas where health and beauty packages include everything from reiki and reflexology to stone therapy and shiatsu. For the ultimate in personal pampering, try any the following hotels: Residence (tel: 415 5888); Telfair (tel: 601 5500); and Heritage (tel: 601 1500). All have state-of-the-art facilities and an atmosphere with a definite 'wow' factor. For dedicated ayurvedic treatment try the Surya Ayurvedic Spa Centre (tel: 263 1637), at Pereybere. Plenty of local beauty parlours also offer treatments at prices well below those charged by the hotels.

## NIGHTLIFE AND ENTERTAINMENT

Most nightlife in Mauritius takes place in the hotels, which stage themed after-dinner shows often featuring the *sega*, a traditional dance imported by African slaves. Sexy and sensual, it

### Tying the Knot in Paradise

Couples seeking the perfect location for their wedding are finding it in increasing numbers among the romantic seascapes and luxury hotels of Mauritius. But before vows can be exchanged, there are some legal necessities to attend to.

To get married on Mauritius, a couple must have a minimum of 24 hours' residency for civil ceremonies and 15 days' residency for religious ceremonies. They must have a valid 10-year passport and bring original birth certificates, decree absolute if divorced and, if getting married within 10 months of the divorce, proof that the bride is not pregnant. Those aged under 18 must have parental consent. If names have been changed by deed poll, legal proof of the change needs to be provided. Once in Mauritius the couple attend the Registrar's Office to sign an affidavit that they are both free to marry. For further information contact the Registrar of Civil Status, 7th floor, Emmanuel Anquetil Building, Port Louis, tel: 201 1727. UK tour operators specialising in weddings are Elite Vacations (<www.elitevacations.com>) and Sunset Faraway Holidays (<www.sunsettravel.com>).

is performed by voluptuous hip-wiggling women and accompanied by musicians beating wildly on the *ravan* (a goatskin tambour), the *maravan* (a hollow tube filled with dried seeds) and the triangle. Rodriguans have their own form of *sega* and traditional music, which you can see at hotels and a three-day Festival Kreol, which takes place at the end of October.

Away from the resorts, nightlife is low-key, apart from several bars and discotheques in Grand Baie, Flic en Flac and Tamarin. Cultural activities are usually poorly advertised, so it can be hard to pin down what's going on. Shows, invariably in French or Creole, are occasionally performed at the Municipal Theatre, Port Louis, and the Swami Vivekananda Conference Centre at Pailles. There are casinos at some of the larger hotels, one at the Caudan Waterfront, a seedy Chinese casino in Port Louis, and one in Curepipe. All the island's cinemas screen English-language films dubbed into French.

**The *sega*, a traditional dance imported by African slaves**

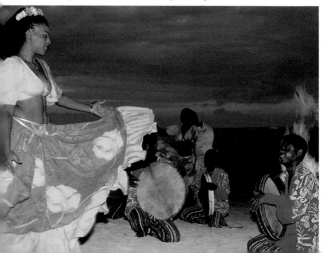

# SHOPPING

Local handicrafts include embroidery, paintings, basketware, model ships, pottery, recycled glassware and toiletries made from locally produced essential oils. Since the closure of many textile factories and increased competition from Asia, jewellery, knitwear and textiles are not the bargains one might expect. Many tour operators organise shopping trips to Port Louis, Floreal and Curepipe, or you can take a taxi and do it yourself. Shops to look out for are: Adamas (tel: 686 5246), Passion (tel: 647 9499) and Cledor (tel: 698 8959), for diamond and precious stones set in fabulous

**Model ships of interest to collectors may be purchased from First Fleet Productions (tel: 698 0161) at Floreal, and Historic Marine (tel: 283 9304) at Goodlands.**

designs; Etoile d'Orient (tel: 686 8280), for duty-free antiques, silks, carpets and jewellery; and Floreal Square (tel: 698 7959), for cashmere and knitted goods. Beachwear and designer clothing under the Harris Wilson, Karl Kaiser, Marina Rinaldi and Max Mara labels are also excellent value.

Shops tend to have fixed prices, but you can test your bargaining skills in markets, of which there are dozens  throughout the island. The most popular is the Central Market at Port Louis, which is renowned for its fresh fruit and vegetables and dozens of stalls selling clothing, spices and souvenirs. More modern European-style retail shopping complexes are found

**Grown on a large scale in Mauritius, anthuriums, with their showy heart-shaped spathes and protruding flower spikes, make distinctive souvenirs or gifts. They are best bought in specially packaged boxes at the airport when you leave.**

at the following locations: Jumbo at Terre Rouge and Phoenix; Sunset Boulevard at Grand Baie; Caudan Waterfront; Trianon; Floreal; and Ruisseau Creole at Tamarin. Curepipe has a range of older-style shopping arcades specialising in Chinese jade, porcelain, silks and upmarket goods. Tailors in Curepipe will also make up an outfit within 48 hours.

Look out for items produced under the Coffret des Îles label. These include a hamper containing local vanilla-flavoured tea, coffee, sugar, spices and fruit, which can be air freighted to your home address within 72 hours. See your hotel receptionist, tel: 637 8383 or visit <www.send-flowers.mu>. Green Island rum, liqueurs and punches made from sugar cane also make good souvenirs, along with luggage-friendly vacuum packs of smoked marlin.

In Rodrigues, mind-blowing bottled chillies and pickles, delicious honey and a range of handicrafts made from coconut and other natural materials make unusual souvenirs. They can be bought from Careco (tel: 831 1766) and other small outlets in Port Mathurin.

## CHILDREN'S MAURITIUS

With many safe bathing beaches and professionally run mini-clubs in the larger hotels, Mauritius is a very child-friendly destination. The slides and chutes of Belle Mare Waterpark (tel: 415 2626) provide hours of fun. At Domaine les Pailles (tel: 286 4225), you can join a horse-drawn carriage tour, visit the mask museum and sugar distillery, and then have lunch at the Dolce Vita restaurant, followed by a dip in the pool.

Animals are always a good bet when the appeal of splashing in seawater and building sandcastles starts to wear thin. Casela Nature and Leisure Park (tel: 452 0693) has a zoo and aviary, while crocodiles and tortoises are star attractions at La Vanille Crocodile Park (tel: 626 2503). For the very young, try a ride in the toy train on the Caudan Waterfront in Port Louis or the interactive displays at L'Aventure de Sucre Museum (tel: 243 0660) at Beau Plan.

Older children with a sense of adventure may like to try their skills and stamina at Parc Aventure, Chamarel (tel: 234 5385), where roped ladders and nets festoon trees and rivers, allowing exciting discoveries in a 12-hectare (30-acre) forest. Alternatively, there is Kart Loisirs (tel: 233 2223) at Petit Riviere, where 35 go-karts equipped with 270cc engines tear around a 900m (3,000ft) course; the swimming pool and restaurant have magnificent views of Port Louis.

**Belle Mare Waterpark**

# Festival Calendar

Many festivals are moveable dates and information on the more unusual events such as fire- and sword-walking, celebrated by the Tamil community, is hard to come by. For more specific information about dates, times and venues of those shown below, contact the tourist office.

**January/February** *Cavadee* A Tamil festival in which devotees pierce their bodies and faces with skewers as an act of penance to the deity, Muruga. *Chinese Spring Festival* Celebration of the Chinese New Year with firecrackers and displays of dragon dances; the Chinese community offer gifts wrapped in red – symbol of happiness – and there is plenty of eating and drinking following prayers at the temples.

**February/March** *Maha Shivaratree* A celebration by the Hindu community, in honour of Lord Shiva, in which thousands of devotees dressed in white leave their homes in all corners of the island and walk to Grand Bassin, a lake which they believe to be linked to the River Ganges. *Holi* A lively, two-day Hindu festival during which unsuspecting passersby get squirted with coloured water and powder, which is supposed to bring good luck.

**March/April** *Ougadi* A low-key New Year festival celebrated by the small minority of Hindu Telegus.

**15 August** *Assumption Day* Rodrigues' main Christian festival is marked by a huge outdoor mass before the statue of the Virgin Mary at La Reine de Rodrigues, just outside Port Mathurin.

**9 September** Mauritians of all denominations walk or drive to the tomb of Père Laval at Sainte-Croix, just outside Port Louis, to celebrate the priest's healing powers.

**October/November** *Divali*, or *the Festival of Light* The Hindu community lights the entire island with small clay lamps and candles, signifying the triumph of good over evil.

*Eid ul Fitr* Muslims celebrate the end of Ramadam, the month of fasting. The date varies from year to year according to the lunar calendar, and the exact date depends on the sighting of a full moon.

# EATING OUT

Food lovers are in for a treat in Mauritius, thanks to a cuisine that's as diverse as the country's people. Wherever you dine you'll find food reflecting influences from India, China, Africa and Europe, from spicy curries and noodles to a melange of exotic fruit and vegetables, sumptuous seafood, and not forgetting the basic burger and chips.

Virtually every restaurant has Indian, Chinese, Creole and European food on its menu and if you don't know what to start with, simply ask for *gadjaks*, which are an assortment of hot snacks such as *croquettes*, croustillants (crispy balls) made from meat, fish, chicken or vegetables, or *gateaux piments* (chilli cakes). Mauritians nibble throughout the day on *gadjaks* and eat large amounts of rice.

**Perfect presentation**

Local beef and lamb is not as tender as the imported cuts from South Africa, Australia and New Zealand, but home-reared chicken and pork is plentiful and good. With the majority of the population being of the Hindu faith, vegetarians are well catered for. Half the fun of eating out is identifying the amazing variety of fruit and vegetables.

You can choose to eat cheaply at roadside stalls, stick to your hotel, or venture into the resorts and villages where a whole range of restaurants dish up tasty meals at knock-down prices. If you are on an all-inclusive deal, try at least a couple of outside restaurants if only to rub shoulders with the locals and tuck into authentic Mauritian fare. People tend to eat fairly early in the evening, and restaurants are often closed by 10pm.

## WHAT TO EAT

### Indian

Cooks grind herbs and spices to make a *massala*, which is then used with meat, chicken, fish or vegetables to produce delicious curries. Particularly tasty are the *vindaye* curries, made from wine or vinegar and garlic. Some curries are hotter than others, depending on the ingredients used. Plain boiled or saffron-flavoured rice is always served along with chilli sauce. If the curry is too hot, don't drink water but mop up the sauce with rice or bread. Indian breads include thick rounds of *roti* (similar to *naan*),

**Coquelet tandoori**

which can be plain or stuffed, or the finer version called *faratha*. A typical Muslim dish is the rice-based *briyani* (biriyani), which is flavoured with a subtle blend of spices and spiked with meat, fish, chicken or vegetables.

Commonly eaten by all Mauritians, *dhall puri* is an Indian snack that is virtually a meal in itself. Best

**Service with a smile**

eaten at roadside stalls in resorts, villages and markets because it is freshly made to order, these gut-busting floury pancakes are made with crushed lentils and come stuffed with a tomato, onion and garlic-flavoured sauce called *rougaille*, or any filling you fancy. The luminous green chilli sauce is optional but a smattering gives it that extra bite. *Puris*, on the other hand, are lighter, tiny disc-shaped pancakes, which can be filled with tasty portions of vegetable or meat curry. Try also *gateaux piments* (chilli cakes) and *samoussas* (curry-filled pastries) fresh from the pan.

## Chinese

Chinese dishes are varied and very good value. For something fast and easy, ask for a *mine frite* (fried noodles). If you're feeling adventurous or especially hungry ask for a *mine frite special*, which includes eggs, seafood, chicken or meat. A lighter version that is not unlike vermicelli is *meefoon*. Try also *bol renversee*, an upturned bowl of rice, stabbed with slivers of pork, spicy sausage and chunky chicken, or *fooyang*, an omelette-based offering filled with lobster, crab or prawns. Exotic dishes such as shark-fin soup, sea cucumber and Peking duck are the preserve of upmarket restaurants and should be ordered in advance. Chefs use lots of *ajinomoto* (MSG or monosodium gluta-mate) to enhance flavour.

## Creole

Creole food is best described as a fiery fusion of Indian, Chinese and French cuisine; it is traditionally spicy. The end result depends on the whims and imagination of the cook. Culinary wonders emerge from the cooking pot in the form of rich meat and fish *daubes* (casseroles) and *caris* (curries), helped along with the ubiquitous chilli and a cornucopia of herbs and spices. Venison and wild boar are especially good, and plenty of seafood, including octopus and squid, are served in this way, along with a huge variety of local fish, which are usually grilled or fried. Among the exotic vegeta-bles are *coeur de palmist* (palm hearts), known as mil-lionaire's salad; *gros pois* (butter beans); *bredes* (fresh greens); and *lentilles noires* (black lentils). Pumpkin and marrow are also popular. As an accompaniment, you may be offered *achards* or pick-led grated vegetables, which are served in tiny dishes.

> For obvious reasons, fish dishes feature strongly in this island nation's cuisine. Species you may find on the menu include *vieille rouge* (grouper), *carangue* (trevally), *cordonnier* (surgeon fish), *cateaux* (parrot fish), *bourgeois* (red snapper), *capitaine* (white snapper) and *licorne* (unicorn fish).

**Sweet delights**

## Desserts

Desserts in restaurants are usually fresh fruits of the season, ice creams or sweet pancakes, while hotel buffets include a huge variety of European-style sticky pastries, fancy puddings, cakes and cheeses. Summer fruits include mangoes, lychees, water melon and passion fruit, and year round there is plenty of pawpaw, pineapple and banana. Indian sweets are reserved for special occasions, although you can sometimes buy them at patisseries and supermarkets. At Chinese New Year, small, round waxy cakes called *gateaux cirées* are served.

## Rodriguan Specialities

The lagoons of Rodrigues provide a natural larder for the islanders, most of whom are fisherfolk. Fish and other seafood are served in hotel and local restaurants in Port Mathurin. Octopus is used in salads, *cari* (curry) and

**Lychees fresh from the tree**

*daube* (casserole), and is less expensive than lobster, prawn and crab, which are simply steamed. Another local speciality is *cono cono*, a mollusc similar to whelk, which is incorporated into a refreshing salad dressed with local limes. Fresh fish is jazzed up and fried Chinese-style with ginger and garlic. *Cari de poulet aux grains* (chicken curry with red beans) and *poisson salé* (salt fish) are typical Rodriguan dishes served with plain boiled rice. Go easy on the local *achards* (pickles) since they are made from chillies that are considerably stronger than the ones that are grown in Mauritius.

Desserts are not really eaten and fresh fruit is rare, but you can find plenty of shops selling *pain frit* (fried bread sprinkled with sugar), *gateau patate* (sweet potato cake), *gateau manioc* (manioc cake) and *pudding mais* (maize pudding). All drinks, including beer, soft drinks and water, are imported from Mauritius.

# WHERE TO EAT

Most of the luxury hotels tend to be in isolated locations, and dining in local restaurants often involves a taxi ride. Hotel food is plentiful and varied, although often toned down to cater for international tastes. The larger hotels often have several eateries, usually a main buffet-style one and one or more à la carte or beach restaurants. Some hotels have separate facilities for children.

**Barbecue on the boat**

Many local restaurants may seem oddly located to the visitor, squeezed between, above or behind ramshakle buildings, tucked behind petrol-station forecourts, or hidden deep in the cane fields. The décor may be quirky and the service, although friendly and welcoming, may not always come up

## Lunch with the Locals

Some islanders are happy to prepare and serve lunch to visitors in their own homes. This option, known as *table d'hôte*, makes an interesting alternative to traditional restaurant dining and can be booked through Espace Aventure (tel: 670 4301). The food may be Indian, Chinese or Creole, or a mixture of all three, and the experience gives a unique insight into local culinary traditions. In Rodrigues, where the *table d'hôte* concept is more common than in Mauritius, details of participating islanders' homes can be obtained from the Association of Rodriguan Tour Operators (ARTO; tel: 831 3350).

to standard. However, the food is fresh and tasty. The more expensive restaurants have air conditioning, tasteful furnishings and pleasant views.

Most top tourist attractions, such as the Domaine du Chasseur, Eureka, l'Aventure de Sucre, and Casela Leisure and Nature Park, have their own restaurants set in gorgeous locations. These tend to be heavily booked by tour groups, but there is nothing to stop you from making a reservation or, in some cases, just turning up.

Several colonial houses have been restored to their former grandeur and serve a typical Creole lunch of smoked marlin, palm-heart salad, venison or seafood, in stylish surroundings. Try Le Ravin at Eureka, Mon Repos at Trianon, Le Jardin de Beau Vallon at Mahebourg, and St Aubin. Reservations are recommended.

There are sophisticated Thai, Japanese and Italian restaurants in the Grand Baie area. Fast-food courts in shopping malls also do a roaring trade in local and international fare. Try the food courts at the Caudan Waterfront in Port Louis, Trianon, Jumbo at Riche Terre, Super U at Grand Baie, and the trendy Ruisseau Creole complex at Tamarin.

## DRINKS

Local beers include the Blue Marlin, Stella and Phoenix brands. Rum comes in two varieties, white and dark. The best brand of rum is Green Island, which can be drunk neat or as a cocktail. Cheaper versions to look for are Mainstay Dry Cane Spirit, Goodwill and Old Mill. There are some quite palatable red, white and rosé wines made locally from imported grape concentrate.

> If you are invited into a Mauritian home, you may be offered a glass of *rhum arrangé*, a rum-based concoction in which fruits and spices have been left to macerate for months.

Labels to look for are Eureka, Chateau Bel Ombre and Saint Nicholas. Australian, New Zealand and South African wines are good value, unlike French wines, champagne and spirits, which are expensive. A good range of potent alcoholic fruit cocktails is also available.

Whisky is also produced locally. Imported blended Scotch whisky is expensive compared with the local King Robert and Findlater brands.

Non-alcoholic drinks include *alouda*. This is made from *agar agar* (boiled china grass) and sugar, soaked *tookmaria* (sweet basil) seeds and flavoured with milk and

**Local rum is popular**

rose water. You will also find the usual range of soft drinks and bottled mineral water. Milky, vanilla-flavoured tea with plenty of sugar is widely drunk, although black tea is also available. Coffee comes as *espresso*, filter or *cappuccino*, but in small snack bars and restaurants you are more likely to be served with the instant chicory-flavoured version.

Finally, it's wise to drink plenty of water. The ubiquitous 'traveller's tummy', blamed so often on 'dodgy' food, is more likely to be the result of drinking too little water. In Mauritius, especially when it is hot and humid, dehydration is an all too common cause of many stomach complaints, so always carry water with you. Fortunately, it's plentiful and cheap and can be bought in all food shops and petrol stations.

## To Help You Order...

| | |
|---|---|
| Could we have a table? | **Je voudrais une table.** |
| I'd like a/an/some... | **Je voudrais…** |
| The bill, please. | **L'addition s'il vous plait.** |

| | | | |
|---|---|---|---|
| bread | **pain** | pepper | **poivre** |
| butter | **buerre** | potatoes | **pommes de terre** |
| coffee | **café** | rice | **riz** |
| dessert | **desert** | salad | **salade** |
| fish | **poisson** | salt | **sel** |
| fruit | **fruit** | sandwich | **sandwich** |
| ice cream | **glace** | soup | **soupe** |
| meat | **viande** | sugar | **sucre** |
| menu | **carte** | tea | **thé** |
| milk | **lait** | wine | **vin** |

*Bourgeois* – red snapper fish

## ... and Read the Menu

| | |
|---|---|
| achards | pickled vegetables |
| agneau | lamb |
| ail | garlic |
| ananas | pineapple |
| bourgeois | red snapper fish |
| bredes | fresh greens |
| camaron | shrimp/prawns |
| capitaine | white snapper |
| carangue | trevally fish |
| cari cerf | venison curry |
| cateaux | parrot fish |
| champignons | mushrooms |
| cochon marron | wild boar |
| coeur de palmist | palm hearts |
| cordonnier | surgeon fish |
| crabe | crab |
| daube | stewed or casseroled- |
| desert | dessert |
| entrecote | beef rib steak |
| filet | fillet |
| fruits de mer | seafood |
| gros pois | butter beans |
| haricots | beans |
| jambon | ham |
| kalamar | squid |
| legumes | vegetables |
| lentilles noires | black lentils |
| licorne | unicorn fish |
| marlin fumé | smoked marlin |
| melon d'eau | watermelon |
| ourite | octopus |
| petit pois | peas |
| poisson salé | salt fish |
| pommes d'amour | tomatoes |
| poulet/ poisson croustillant | crispy fried chicken/fish balls |
| riz blanc | boiled rice |
| riz saffran | saffron-flavoured rice |
| rougaille | tomato, onion and garlic flavoured sauce |
| sauce piment | chilli sauce |
| saucisse chinoise | spicy Chinese sausage |
| thon | tuna |
| vieille rouge | grouper fish |
| vindaye | curry dish based on vinegar or wine and garlic |

# HANDY TRAVEL TIPS

*An A–Z Summary of Practical Information*

# A

## ACCOMMODATION

Hotels in Mauritius are not ranked according to a star-rating system. Nevertheless, many hotels, including the less grand ones, undergo frequent refurbishment and are of a consistently high standard with service to match. Typical facilities include restaurants, bars, swimming pools, mini-clubs, air conditioning and satellite TV. Don't just turn up and expect to get a room or use the facilities as a non-guest, especially during July, Christmas and New Year, when rooms are pre-booked by overseas tour operators. All beach hotels offer free water-sports, with the exception of big-game fishing and scuba diving, and many have diving schools.

Hotels owned and managed by companies such as Beachcomber (<www.beachcomber-hotels.com>), Sun International (<www.sun-resorts.com>), Naiade (<www.naiade.com>), Indigo (<www.indigohotels.com>) and Veranda (<www.veranda-resorts.com>) are in stunning, often isolated, beach locations.

Increasingly popular with repeat visitors is staying in self-catering accommodation in the main resorts of Grand Baie and Flic en Flac. Generally, the rate you pay depends on distance from the beach and/or your length of stay; the cheapest options are for units some distance from the beach rented for long periods. While these units should be registered with the tourist office, many are not, and you may find that basic safety and security measures don't measure up to Western standards. Always inspect the rooms before committing yourself. Reputable companies with a wide selection of accommodation are Jet's Villas (<www.jet-7.com>), Mauritours (<www.mauritours.net>) and Elegant Destinations (<www.elegantdestinations.co.uk>).

Those wanting a change from sun, sea and sand should look for eco-lodges and traditional rural bungalows. Useful sites to visit are <www.dchasseur.com>, <www.ecuriecheminee.com>, <www.maisoneureka.com> and <www.tropicscope.com>.

There are no official camping sites.

| | |
|---|---|
| Do you have a single/ double room? | **Avez-vous une chambre simple/double?** |
| I would like to reserve a room with double bed/twin beds and bath/shower. | **Je voudrais réserver une chambre avec grand lit/deux lits et bain/douche.** |
| Is the hotel air conditioned? | **Est-ce que l'hôtel est climatisé?** |
| Is breakfast included? | **Est-ce que le petit déjeuner est compris?** |

## AIRPORT (see also GETTING THERE)

Sir Seewoosagur Ramgoolam International Airport, locally referred to as SSR (tel: 637 3420), is at Plaisance, 48km (30 miles) south of the capital, Port Louis. You can buy a reasonable range of good-value duty-free items on arrival. If you are on a package holiday, your tour rep will meet you and arrange transfer to your hotel. There are no direct buses to the tourist resorts, so independent travellers will have to take a taxi. Agree a fare before accepting a ride, and expect to pay around R1,500 for the journey to Grand Baie. Departure and tourist taxes are included in the cost of your air ticket.

# B

## BICYCLE HIRE

Bicycles and helmets in good condition can be rented from the more upmarket hotels. Hotels can also organise guided cycle tours of the island, particularly in the north, which lends itself to some easy rides. Most resorts have bikes for hire, but check brakes and tyres as they are not always in good condition. Punctures can be easily repaired at a tyre repair shop, found in most villages.

## BUDGETING FOR YOUR TRIP

Expect to pay handsomely for all those extras if you confine yourself to a hotel. In the real world, basics are remarkably cheap and nearly everything is paid for in Mauritian rupees. Sixty rupees are worth approximately £1 sterling or US$2.

**Getting there**. Because there are few charter flights, airfares are a major expense, especially if coming from Europe or the US. Low-season flights from major European destinations start at around £600, although package deals through your tour operator can sometimes work out only fractionally higher than the airfare.

**Accommodation**. The sky's the limit at the posh beach-resort hotels where you can expect to pay European prices and more. A mid-range hotel costs around R4,000 a night for a double room with breakfast and dinner. Self-catering options are very good value, ranging between R1,000 and R3,000 a day for an apartment or villa.

**Meals and drinks**. Eating out is cheap. A simple meal and soft drink or beer will cost less than R250 per person. The cost of meals in the most expensive non-hotel restaurants compares favourably with European prices. Seafood, excluding lobster, is plentiful and cheap. Imported alcohol and wine can double the bill.

**Local transport**. Although taxis have meters, these are rarely used, so agree a price for the trip beforehand. Prices for short journeys are on a par with UK prices, although better deals can be struck for half-day (R1,500) or full-day hire (R2,500). Buses are cheap and plentiful, but in resort areas they stop operating after 7pm. Car hire starts from R1,200 a day. Petrol costs R40 per litre (2007).

**Watersports**. Scuba-diving packages of five and 10 dives are around R3,600 and R7,000 respectively. Experienced divers can expect to pay around R800 for a day dive and R1,000 for a night dive. A day on a big-game fishing boat costs around R9,000 per person. Hotel guests can expect free water sports, including wind-surfing, snorkelling, water skiing, glass-bottom boat trips, pedalos and, in some cases, hobie cats.

# C

## CAR HIRE (see also DRIVING)

Rates include insurance, collision damage waiver and discounts depending on length of hire. Credit cards are accepted and you will be asked to sign a blank voucher for the deposit, which will be destroyed in your presence when you return the car. Cars can be collected at the airport or at any pre-arranged point and dropped off when you leave. The more expensive companies are the international ones: Avis (tel: 208 6031), Europcar (tel: 286 0140) and Hertz (tel: 670 4301). Less expensive operators are: Allocar (tel: 631 1810), Arnulfy and Co. (tel: 631 9806) and JR Car Rental (tel: 254 1142).

| | |
|---|---|
| I'd like to rent a car | **Je voudrais louer une voiture** |
| now/tomorrow | **tout de suite/demain** |
| for one day/a week | **pour une journée/une semaine** |

## CLIMATE

Mauritius has a tropical maritime climate. There are two seasons, summer and winter. Summer, from November to April, is hot and humid, with short bursts of heavy rain and the occasional cyclone. Winter, from May to October, is pleasant and dry, nights are cooler and there is less humidity than in summer. The southeast trade winds blow all year, keeping the south and east coasts fresher during the summer, but it can get uncomfortably windy at other times. On the coast expect daytime temperatures of 20–25°C (68–77°F) in winter and 25–34°C (77–93°F) in summer. The chart below shows maximum average daytime temperatures in Port Louis.

| | J | F | M | A | M | J | J | A | S | O | N | D |
|---|---|---|---|---|---|---|---|---|---|---|---|---|
| °C | 30 | 29 | 29 | 28 | 26 | 24 | 24 | 24 | 25 | 27 | 28 | 29 |
| °F | 86 | 84 | 84 | 82 | 79 | 75 | 75 | 75 | 77 | 81 | 82 | 84 |

**Cyclones**. The cyclone season is between December and April. Cyclones, powerful tropical storms, start hundreds of kilometres away to the northeast of Mauritius and take days to move westwards. Weather stations in the Indian Ocean track their route and warnings are broadcast days in advance. Cyclones vary in strength, some merely bringing heavy rains and winds, but others can have devastating effects, resulting in damage to buildings and cuts to the power and water supply. All hotels have their own generators and are well equipped to deal with a cyclone. When red warning flags are flown from public buildings you should not venture out. Local radio and TV stations broadcast regular bulletins. Always comply with directions or advice. For cyclone information, tel: 96; recorded weather information, tel: 302 6071.

## CLOTHING

Loose cotton shorts, shirts, T-shirts and dresses are ideal for the balmy climate of Mauritius. Men should wear a collared shirt and trousers at dinner in upmarket hotels; a jacket and tie is necessary only for formal functions. Wearing swimsuits in the hotel dining room or in town is likely to offend, while nudity and topless bathing on any beach is a definite no-no. A sturdy pair of walking shoes or boots is essential if you intend to go rock-climbing or hiking on the island.

## COMPLAINTS

Package holidaymakers should inform their local rep and/or ask to see the manager of the accommodation. Complaints against taxi drivers should be made to the National Transport Authority, Victoria Square, Port Louis, quoting the number plate, driver's name and details of the journey. Send copies of other complaints to the Director, Mauritius Tourist Promotion Authority, 11th floor, Air Mauritius Centre, 5 John Kennedy Street, Port Louis.

## CRIME AND SAFETY

Mauritius is a generally low-risk destination. Any crime that does take place is usually opportunistic, so avoid deserted, unlit places, wear a money belt if visiting Port Louis market, don't flaunt expensive jewellery and don't give lifts to strangers. If driving, never leave anything on show in your car and remember to lock doors and windows in self-catering accommodation. All hotels provide free safety deposit boxes.

Sadly, there is one 'no-go area', the slum settlement of Karo Kalyptus, just north of the capital, Port Louis. Motorists have been victims of nasty attacks when forced to slow down on the motorway at the adjacent Roches Bois roundabout.

## CUSTOMS AND ENTRY REQUIREMENTS

Nationals of the EU, USA and all Commonwealth countries do not need visas. Your passport should be valid for six months beyond your arrival date. Entry is normally for a maximum of three months and you will be asked for your return or onward ticket and to provide an address in Mauritius. For longer stays you should go in person to the Immigration Department, Sterling House, Rue Gislet Geoffroy, Port Louis, tel: 210 9312. You will need two passport-size photographs, valid return tickets and evidence of funds to support your stay.

You can bring in the following items duty free: 250 grams of tobacco (including cigars and cigarettes), 1 litre of spirits, 2 litres of wine, ale or beer, 250ml of eau de toilette and a reasonable amount of perfume. Firearms and ammunition must be declared on arrival. Prescription medicines for personal use carried in an official container are permitted. Finally, anyone trying to engage in drug trafficking is likely to find themselves in jail for a very long time.

# D

## DRIVING

**Road conditions**. Most roads are surfaced (some better than others), but if driving through the sugar-cane areas, watch out for deep gullies on either side of the road. Take extra care when driving through villages as accidents, irrespective of whose fault it is, can incur the wrath of the local population. Traffic in towns and villages is generally slow-moving, with cyclists, wandering pedestrians and stray dogs adding to the difficulties. Be warned: Mauritius has one of the highest road-death rates in the world due to badly lit streets, poorly placed road signs, an absence of decent pavements and incompetent driving habits.

**Driving regulations**. Drivers should be over 23 and must at all times carry an international or valid driving licence from their own country to avoid incurring a hefty fine. Drive on the left. Speed limits are 90km/h (60mph) on the motorway and 50km/h (30mph) elsewhere. Distances and speed limits are shown in kilometres and road signs are in English. The wearing of seatbelts is compulsory and there is no age restriction for front-seat passengers. Parking restrictions apply in towns and you should display a parking coupon, available in booklets from petrol stations. If you hire a motorcycle, you must wear a crash helmet. Accidents should be reported on an 'agreed statement of facts' form which is provided with your hire car. Personal-injury accidents must be reported to the police.

**Fuel**. Most filling stations are open from 7am to 7pm. Prices for petrol and diesel compare favourably with those in Europe. Attendants will fill your car and do not expect a tip. Ensure you have cash as credit cards are not accepted.

| | |
|---|---|
| driver's licence | **permis de conduire** |
| car registration papers | **carte grise** |
| Fill the tank, please. | **Le plein, s'il vous plaît.** |
| My car has broken down. | **Ma voiture est en panne.** |
| There's been an accident. | **Il y a eu un accident.** |

## E

### ELECTRICITY

Electrical appliances in hotels operate on 220 volts. Both square three-pin plugs and round two-pin plugs are used on the island, but take an adaptor. Power cuts are frequent, but hotels have their own generators.

### EMBASSIES AND HIGH COMMISSIONS

**Australia**: Rogers House (2nd floor), John Kennedy Street, Port Louis, tel: 208 1700.

**Canada**: c/o Blanche Birger Company Ltd, Jules Koenig Street, Port Louis, tel: 212 5500.

**South Africa**: 4th floor, BAI Building, Pope Hennessy Street, Port Louis, tel: 212 6925.

**UK**: 7th floor, Les Cascades Building, Edith Cavell Street, Port Louis, tel: 208 9850. There is also an Honorary Consul in Port Mathurin, Rodrigues, tel: (230) 832 0120.

**USA**: 4th Floor, Rogers House, John Kennedy Street, Port Louis, tel: 202 4400

## EMERGENCIES (see also MEDICAL CARE and POLICE)

The following numbers are useful 24 hours a day in an emergency:

| | |
|---|---|
| Police | **999** |
| Fire | **995** |
| Ambulance | **114** |

## G

### GAY AND LESBIAN TRAVELLERS

Homosexuality is tolerated in Mauritius, but kissing and canoodling in public places, whether by gays or straights, is not the done thing.

### GETTING THERE (see also AIRPORT)

Most visitors arrive in Mauritius on a packaged scheduled airline deal provided by their home travel agent. Scheduled flights with the national carrier, Air Mauritius, come from Europe, Africa, Asia and Australia. Travellers from the US will need to take a connecting flight. Air Mauritius flies from the following destinations: London, Paris, Frankfurt, Munich, Vienna, Brussels, Geneva, Zurich, Madrid, Rome, Durban, Cape Town, Nairobi, Moroni, Harare, Antananarivo, Seychelles, Hong Kong, Singapore, Kuala Lumpur, Mumbai, Delhi, Perth and Melbourne. Fares from the UK start at around £600.

The only way of getting to Rodrigues is from Mauritius or the French island of Réunion. The flight takes approximately 90 minutes. From Mauritius, the sea voyage aboard the *MV Mauritius Pride* or the *Mauritius Trochettia* takes about 27 hours. Contact the Mauritius Shipping Corporation (tel: 241 2550, fax: 242 5245) or your travel agent.

A French charter company, Corsair, flies from Paris to Mauritius, and other charter flights are destined to follow. An alternative is to take a charter flight from Paris to Réunion booked through Nouvelles Frontiers <www.newfronties.com> and a scheduled flight from there to Mauritius.

Other airlines serving Mauritius are: Air Austral, British Airways, Air France, Air Europe, Emirates, Condor, South African Airways and Singapore Airlines.

## GUIDES AND TOURS

If you're staying in an isolated hotel and want to see the island, the best way is to book a guided tour. Tour operators, such as Mauritours (tel: 467 9700), White Sands (tel: 208 5424) and Summertimes (tel: 427 1111) have hospitality desks at major hotels and can arrange full- and half-day tours in air-conditioned vehicles with multi-lingual guides, as well as sea excursions, helicopter trips and other services. Smaller companies operate in the resort areas, but you should avoid freelance 'guides' on the beaches because they won't have appropriate insurance.

Air Mauritius Helicopter Section (tel: 603 3754, fax: 637 3754) offers regular sightseeing tours. Prices vary depending on flying time and route. Current tariffs start at R18,000 per helicopter, which can accommodate up to four people. Transfers from the airport to your hotel for a maximum of four people are R24,000 per helicopter. Reservations for an airport–hotel transfer should be made before leaving home through your travel agent.

# H

## HEALTH AND MEDICAL CARE

Mauritius is malaria-free and no vaccinations are needed unless coming from an infected area. You should take out travel insurance, but remember that many companies exclude coverage for extreme sports, such as rock-climbing and mountaineering, although you may be covered for quad-biking. If you are contemplating taking part in any sea or land sports, confirm with the tour operator that the activity is within your level, keeping in mind that the operator is in business to make money. You should ask your guide to confirm that he or she is a qualified first-aider and that drinks and first-aid equipment are carried at all times. But most importantly – and this cannot be stressed enough – ask what emergency back-up measures exist in case of accident or sudden illness. Although emergency medical treatment is free in public hospitals, these tend to be overcrowded and understaffed places, and ambulances are poorly equipped. If there is any doubt at all, don't book.

There are plenty of good private clinics that recognise overseas travel-insurance policies *(see page 118)*, so keep all receipts and documentation in the event of a medical claim. The cost of emergency and/or routine treatment is substantially less than in Europe. If you need a doctor or dentist consult your hotel. Most generic medicines are available at pharmacies, which are recognisable by a green cross, but if you are on any special medication it is better to bring your own.

Tap water is generally safe to drink, except during water shortages or cyclone periods, but in case of doubt there is plenty of bottled water available. Tummy upsets should be rare since food in hotels is prepared under strict hygienic conditions. Avoid eating anything that has been left uncovered.

Use a high-factor sun cream, wear a hat, and drink plenty of water to avoid dehydration. Avoid activity during the hottest part of the day. Pack an insect repellent, as mosquitoes can be a nuisance particularly after heavy rains, and carry antihistamine to treat insect bites. Wear protective shoes when exploring the reef and muddy waters. If you should tread on the venomous stonefish seek medical treatment immediately.

**Public Hospitals**. SSR Hospital, Pamplemousses (tel: 243 3661); Moka Eye Hospital, Moka (tel: 433 4015); Doctor Jeetoo Hospital, Port Louis (tel: 212 3201); Princess Margaret Hospital, Quatre Bornes (tel: 425 3031); Jawaharlal Nehru Hospital, Rose Belle (tel: 627 4951). **Private clinics** accepting medical insurance are: Clinique du Nord, Tombeau Bay (tel: 247 2532); Clinique Darné, Floréal (tel: 686 1477); and Med Point Clinic, Quatre Bornes (tel: 426 7777).

## HOLIDAYS

The following are public holidays when all public services are closed:

| | |
|---|---|
| 1 and 2 January | New Year's Day |
| 1 February | Abolition of Slavery Day |
| 12 March | Republic Day |
| 1 May | Labour Day |
| 2 November | All Saints' Day |
| 25 December | Christmas Day |

In addition, there are eight major festivals, mostly with moveable dates, celebrated by the various religions. The date of Eid ul Fitr, marking the end of Ramadan, varies from year to year according to the lunar calendar, and over time can take place in any month.

| | |
|---|---|
| January/February | Chinese Spring Festival |
| Mid-January/February | Cavadee |
| February/March | Maha Shivaratree; Holi |
| March/April | Ougadi |
| 15 August | Assumption Day |
| September | Ganesh Chaturthi |
| October/November | Divali |

On Rodrigues, Chinese-run shops and businesses shut down for about one week during Chinese Spring Festival.

# L

## LANGUAGE

The official language is English, although most people are more comfortable conversing in French. Creole, a form of pidgin French, remains the *lingua franca*. You'll also hear Indian and Chinese languages spoken, such as Bhojpuri (a sort of Creolised Hindi), Tamil, Urdu, Telegu, Marathi, Gujurati, Mandarin and Cantonese. Nearly everyone employed in tourism speaks both English and French.

# M

## MAPS

The tourist office produces a free map, and other reasonable ones can be found in hotel boutiques. The Government of Mauritius publishes the best map, which includes an insert of Rodrigues. In Mauritius it costs around R400 and can be bought in Port Louis at the Caudan Waterfront Bookshop, or the Ministry of Housing, Lands and Environment, 3rd Floor, Edith Cavell Street. An alternative is the French IGN No. 5/15. Both maps are also available in the UK at Stanford's, 12/14 Long Acre, Covent Garden, London WC2E 9LP, tel: 020 7836 1321, <www.stanfords.co.uk>.

## MEDIA

For a country whose official language is English there are surprisingly few publications in English. What books there are tend to be imported and expensive, and current magazines and newspapers are often hard to come by. All local newspapers are in French and include *Le Matinal*, which has a daily lifestyle section in English, and *L'Express*, which has an English supplement on Tuesdays. The only English-language newspaper is the *News on Sunday*, published on Friday, which tends to sell out fast.

The top hotels provide satellite TV. The Mauritius Broadcasting Corporation (MBC) transmits television news in English at 7am, 5.40pm and 9pm, and radio news at 8am, 3pm and 9pm daily. On radio, the BBC World Service is broadcast all day on 1575AM. Local radio stations focusing on pop music, interviews and items of local interest are: Radio 1 on 101.7FM, Radio Plus on 88.6FM and Top FM on 105.7FM.

## MONEY

**Currency**. The currency used is the Mauritian rupee (R). Notes are in denominations of 25, 50, 100, 200, 500, 1,000 and 2,000; coins are R1, R5 and R10 and 5, 10, 20 and 50 cents. There is no restriction on the amount of foreign currency you can bring in to the country, but if you have a surplus of rupees on departure you can convert them to your home currency. Keep all bank receipts as you can only export a maximum of R350.

**Currency exchange**. The rupee is a fluctuating currency, so keep an eye on the daily exchange rates. There are many banks in Grand Baie, Port Louis and at the airport, which offer much better deals on major currencies than in your hotel or through official money-changing shops.

**Credit cards**. Major credit cards are accepted in large supermarkets, more expensive shops and restaurants, top hotels and car-hire companies. Many retail outlets display credit-card symbols but always check that they accept your card before making any purchases. Petrol stations do not accept credit cards at all. Be aware of high costs charged by your bank or credit-card company when using plastic abroad.

**Traveller's cheques**. Most brands of traveller's cheques in major currencies can be cashed at banks and hotels. Always take your passport with you.

ATMs. Mauritius is a mainly cash-based economy and there are scores of automatic teller machines at banks, supermarkets and shopping complexes throughout the island.

| | |
|---|---|
| Do you accept traveller's cheques/ this credit card? | **Acceptez-vous les chèques de voyage/cette carte de crédit?** |

# O

## OPENING TIMES

**Shops**: Shops in Port Louis are open weekdays 9am–5pm and Saturdays 9am–noon. In the plateau towns most shops close at noon on Thursdays. Port Louis Municipal Market is open Monday to Saturday 6am–6pm and Sunday 6am–noon. The small corner shops or boutiques are open daily 6am–6pm.

**Businesses and offices**: Weekdays 8am–4.30pm; some businesses are open on Saturday morning 9am–noon. Government offices are open weekdays 9am–4pm, closing for lunch between 11.15am and noon.

**Post offices**: Weekdays 8.15am–4pm; Saturdays 8am–11.45am.

**Banks**: Monday–Thursday 9am–3.30pm; Friday 9am–4pm. Closed Saturday and Sunday.

**Museums**: Hours vary greatly. Some close for one or two days a week and at weekends. Check before making a long journey.

**Restaurants**: Restaurants do not keep late hours and last orders should be made before 9pm. Many close on Mondays.

# P

## POLICE

Most police officers on Mauritius are friendly and keen to help visitors to the island. English is spoken at all police stations and there are specially trained tourist police in Grand Baie. If you should become a victim of crime, report the details to the police immediately and insist on either a copy of the report or reference number for your insurance purposes. The police emergency number is **999**.

The police generally leave tourists alone, but if you are driving always carry your licence in case of random checks. There is also a strong presence of police on the 'motorway' where speeding is common and offenders instantly fined.

| | |
|---|---|
| Where's the nearest police station? | **Ou se trouve le commissariat de police le plus proche?** |

## POST OFFICES

On Mauritius, post offices are the only place where you can buy stamps and post letters. Registered parcels to overseas destinations are checked before being sent, so don't seal them until presenting them at the post-office counter. The price for sending a small postcard to Europe is R10. Mail for other destinations should be weighed. Delivery normally takes between three and 10 days. Parcels received in Mauritius from overseas are always checked by customs and must be collected in person at Post Office Headquarters, Quay Street, Port Louis, tel: 208 2851; remember to take your passport with you.

The main post office in Port Louis is at Victoria Square, tel: 208 2434. Post offices are open weekdays 8.15am–4pm; Saturdays 8am–11.45am.

## PUBLIC TRANSPORT

**Buses**. Buses are reliable, cheap and plentiful, even if some are rather dilapidated and slow. During the week they are crowded from 8am to 9am and 4pm to 5pm, but at other times, bus travel can be a pleasant experience and a way of rubbing shoulders with the local people. There are two bus stations in Port Louis: Immigration Square (tel: 242 1425), serving the north, and Victoria Station (tel: 212 1174), serving the plateau towns and the south. Fares range between R16 and R25, or up to R50 if travelling by air-conditioned express service. Conductors will baulk at notes, so always carry small change. Queues are orderly and you buy your ticket on board.

Buses operate in the resorts from 6.30am to 6.30pm, elsewhere from 5.30am to 8pm, with the last bus leaving at 11pm from Port Louis to Curepipe via the plateau towns.

**Taxis**. Taxis are metered, but drivers rarely use them unless you insist. If you think you can make a deal, always agree a price before accepting a ride. Licensed taxis can be hired from taxi stands in town and outside most hotels, or just ask your receptionist. The hotels have a special arrangement with the drivers, who are expected to charge reasonable rates. If you feel you are being overcharged, warn the driver that you will report him to the hotel. This strategy normally works.

Taxis are recognisable by black registration numbers on white plates. Avoid the unlicensed taxis *(taxis marrons)*, which are instantly recognisable because they are nothing more than private cars that have white numbers on black plates. Rates may be low but they are not insured to carry passengers.

Taxis can be hired for a full or half day and are often cheaper than hiring a car to drive yourself. Most drivers make amiable guides and hope to retain your custom by giving you a personal business card. Drivers do not expect to be tipped.

# R

## RELIGION

Just over half the population (52 percent) are Hindu, 28 percent are Christian, predominantly Roman Catholic, and some 16 percent practise Islam. Chinese faiths are also celebrated. Some religious festivals are also public holidays and reflect the religious tolerance of Mauritius's multicultural society. When visiting temples or mosques, remove your shoes and cover arms and legs. In Rodrigues the main religion is Roman Catholicism with most churches being in Port Mathurin (where there is also a Hindu temple and a mosque).

Services in English are held as follows: Roman Catholic Mass on Saturday at St Joseph's Chapel, Celicourt Antelme Street, Rose Hill (tel: 464 2944); Church of England service every Sunday at 8.30am (except the second Sunday of each month) at St Paul's Church, La Caverne, Vacoas (tel: 686 4819); Presbyterian service at St Columba's Church, Phoenix (tel: 696 4404). On Rodrigues, St Barnabas Church in Jenner Street holds an English-language service once a month on Sundays at 8.30am.

# T

## TELEPHONE

The cheapest way to phone overseas is to buy a pre-paid Sezam phone card and, for local calls, the Complis card. Both cards are widely available in units of R150 and R250 (VAT excluded). They give you a lot of talk time at low fixed charges and can be used on any conventional phone. As in the rest of the world, if you use your hotel phone you will incur hefty surcharges. Pay phones are cheaper to use from 10pm to 6am Monday to Friday, from noon to 6am on Saturday and all day Sunday. You can find phone booths taking cards and coins at police stations, post offices, shops and supermarkets. In Port Louis, there are telephone booths at Mauritius Telecom Offices at Rogers House, John Kennedy Street, or at Mauritius Telecom Tower at Edith Cavell Street. Both are open 8.30am to 5pm weekdays; Saturdays 8.30am to 2pm.

The international dialling code for Mauritius and Rodrigues is 230. To call home from Mauritius and/or Rodrigues, dial the international dialling code, 020, followed by your country code, the area code and then the local number, omitting any initial zero.

All local numbers have seven digits. Simply dial the number for connection. In case of difficulty or if you need directory enquiries, contact the operator on 150.

## TIME ZONES

Mauritius is four hours ahead of Greenwich Mean Time (GMT).

| New York | London | Jo'burg | **Mauritius** | Sydney |
|----------|--------|---------|---------------|--------|
| 7am | noon | 2pm | 4pm | 10pm |

## TIPPING

Tipping is not compulsory, but if you have received good service any tips will be appreciated. A service charge of 10 percent is normally included in restaurant bills; ask if you are unsure. Airport porters may demand a tip to get you out of the airport and into a taxi, in which case R25 will do. Taxi drivers do not expect tips.

| Is service included? | **Est-ce que le servis est compris?** |
|----------------------|---------------------------------------|

## TOILETS

Public toilets have improved in recent years but there are still some pretty dire ones at bus stations and markets, which are to be

used in emergencies only. Best of the bunch are inside the Caudan Waterfront complex in Port Louis and those found in big
supermarkets and shopping complexes. Most public beaches also
have adequate toilets. In emergencies you can always use the toilet in a café or restaurant. Carrying your own toilet paper is
highly recommended.

## TOURIST INFORMATION

The Mauritius Tourism Promotion Authority (MTPA) has the following offices abroad:

**Australia**: Mauritius High Commission, 2 Beale Crescent, Deakin,
Canberra, ACT 2600, tel: 061 282 4436, fax: 061 282 3235.
**UK**: 32–33 Elvaston Place, London, SW7 5NW, tel: 020 7584
3666, fax: 020 7225 1135.
**US** and **Canada**: Tourist information can be obtained from the Mauritius Embassy, Suite 441, 4301 Connecticut Avenue NW, Washing-
ton DC 20008, tel: (202) 244 1491/92, fax: (202) 966 0983 or by
visiting the official tourist-office website at <www.mauritius.net>.

On Mauritius, getting reliable information is not always easy. The
only tourist office is located in the capital in a small office on the
ground floor of Air Mauritius Centre, John Kennedy Street, Port
Louis, tel: 210 1545, fax: 212 5142. Even then their stock of
English-language material is poorly written and supplies are erratic,
and you may have to rely on hotels and travel agents whose func-
tion is to sell accommodation and tours. Arriving passengers may
do a little better at the airport where there is an office (tel: 637
3635), which opens during arrivals and departures. There is no
tourist office on Rodrigues.

| | |
|---|---|
| Where's the nearest tourist office? | **Où se trouve le syndicat d'initiative/ de tourisme le plus proche?** |

# W

## WEBSITES AND INTERNET CAFÉS

There are a number of useful websites giving information for people intending to visit Mauritius:

<**www.airmauritius.com**> – comprehensive information on all services offered by Air Mauritius.

<**www.mauritius.net**> – official tourist website for Mauritius and Rodrigues with plenty of useful information.

<**www.mauritiustourism.co.uk**> – the UK-based Mauritius Tourism Promotion Authority's website includes information on getting married in Mauritius.

<**www.mauritian-wildlife.org**> – for information on Mauritian fauna.

<**www.meteo.fr**> – click on Réunion for information on cyclonic activity in the southwestern Indian Ocean.

<**www.primeminister.gov.mu**> – official government website.

<**www.rodrigues-island.org**> – a good site for Rodrigues-related travel information.

**Internet cafés**: Internet cafés are springing up in many tourist resorts and most towns on Mauritius. Rates for 30 minutes' surfing vary between R20 and R50. There are cyber cafés at the following locations:

Cyber Angel, Royal Road, near Police Station, Triolet, tel: 790 1554.
Netshop, Super U Commercial Centre, Grand Baie, tel: 263 0822.
Cyber Ryder, Telecom Tower,Port Louis, tel: 203 7277.
Cyber 2000, Continent Commercial Centre, Phoenix, tel: 698 5473.

## WEIGHTS AND MEASURES

Mauritius uses the metric system.

## Recommended Hotels

The most stylish accommodation is owned and managed by major Mauritian hotel companies, such as Beachcomber, Sun International, Indigo Resorts, Veranda Resorts and Naiade. A growing option is the all-inclusive stay, normally bookable through your home travel agent. The following guide indicates prices for a double room with breakfast during low season. A higher price rating does not necessarily indicate that accommodation and service are superior, but has more to do with number of facilities and proximity and access to exceptionally well-maintained beaches. Locally known as *pieds dans l'eau* these properties command higher prices than those just a few blocks inland. Remember to add 15 percent VAT when budgeting for your accommodation.

| | |
|---|---|
| **$$$$** | over R10,000 |
| **$$$** | R5,000–R10,000 |
| **$$** | R3,000–R5,000 |
| **$** | below R3,000 |

## PORT LOUIS

**Labourdonnais Waterfront $$$$** *Caudan Waterfront, tel: 202 4000, fax: 202 4040, <www.labourdonnais.com>.* Port Louis' flagship business-class hotel, named after the founder of the capital, hogs the best position on the waterfront. The tastefully decorated rooms have gorgeous mountain and harbour views. Open-door policy attracts non-residents to its three restaurants and elegant bar.

**St Georges $$** *19 Rue St Georges, tel: 211 2581, fax: 211 0885.* Unpretentious 60-roomed hotel in a quiet part of the city appealing to short-stay business and leisure travellers. The simple restaurant serves Creole and European fare.

**Le Suffren $$$** *Caudan Waterfront, tel: 202 4900, fax 202 4040, <www.lesuffrenhotel.com>.* Named after a French admiral, this 100-room hotel opened in 2004. There's a distinct nautical atmosphere with swimming pool and artificial beach giving views over the capital. Trendy bar and á la carte restaurant attract a hip Friday-night crowd. Complimentary beach trips and water taxi to its sister hotel, the Labourdonnais.

## THE NORTH

**Bruyere $** *Beach Lane, Pereybere, tel: 263 7316*. Run by a welcoming Scottish woman and her Mauritian husband, this charming complex of simple one- and two-bedroom units is situated in a quiet lane just a short stroll from the beach.

**Calodyne Sur Mer $$** *Mirabelle Avenue, Coastal Road, Calodyne, tel: 282 1590, fax: 282 1363, <www.calodynecarolinegroup. com>*. Bright and cheerful complex of two-storey colonial-style bungalows set in gardens overlooking Coin de Mire Island. Bungalows equipped with microwave and fridge. Kids' club, à la carte restaurant and bar.

**The Oberoi $$$$** *Baie aux Tortues, Pointe aux Piments, tel: 204 3600, fax: 204 3625, <www.oberoihotels.com>*. A small, elegant and highly sophisticated place, strictly the preserve of honeymooners and the occasional A-list celebrity seeking absolute calm. Superbly furnished individual villas, some with plunge pool and high-walled outdoor bathrooms, guarantee privacy. Open-sided silver-service restaurant overlooks a white sandy beach, and Balinese-style statues adorn two pools.

**Paradise Cove $$$** *Anse La Raie, tel: 204 4000, fax: 204 4040, <www.paradisecovehotel.com>*. Small and luxurious retreat in a remote location overlooking Coin de Mire Island. Superb à la carte restaurant, spa and gorgeous private white beach. Popular with honeymooners. Dive centre.

**Paul et Virginie $$** *Coast Road, Grand Gaube, tel: 288 0215, fax: 288 9233, <www.veranda-resorts.com>*. All-inclusive option and authentic colonial atmosphere make this a firm favourite with

Europeans. Two swimming pools, fine seafood and buffet restaurant, intimate bar and 81 comfortable sea-facing rooms.

**Rocksheen Villa $** *161 Morcellement Jubhoo, Trou aux Biches, tel/fax: 265 5043, <www.rocksheenvilla.com>*. Six simple, air-conditioned self-catering apartments run by friendly Scottish/Mauritian couple. Excellent value, homely atmosphere and only 300m (300yds) from a public beach.

**Veranda $$** *Grand Baie, tel: 209 8000, fax: 263 7369, <www.veranda-resorts.com>*. Warm tropical décor reflects an authentic Mauritian lifestyle at this cosy ocean-fronted hideaway. Choice of 20 bungalows and apartments with kitchenette, plus 74 well-equipped standard rooms, poolside dining, mini-club for 4–12 year olds, tennis courts and sweeping views of the bay.

**Le Victoria $$$** *Pointe aux Piments, tel: 204 2000, fax: 261 8224.* Spacious, tropical-style Beachcomber-owned property spanning hundreds of metres of beach protected by a lagoon. Watersports, nightly entertainment, friendly staff and three restaurants make this a good choice for empty nesters, families and business people.

**Villas Mon Plaisir $** *Royal Road, Pointe aux Piments, tel: 261 7471, fax: 261 6600, <www.villasmonplaisir.com>*. Charming family-run complex of two-storey units in pleasant gardens with pool situated on the edge of the village and right on the beach. Welcoming restaurant and bar. Free watersports and dive centre.

## THE EAST

**Beau Rivage $$$$** *Belle Mare, tel: 402 2000, fax: 415 2020, <www.naiade.com>*. This is an eminently chic retreat appealing to honeymooners, couples and families. The bar and restaurant overlooks a gorgeous pool and beach. Wonderful spa, nightly entertainment, free watersports and mini-club for 3–11 year olds.

**Belle Mare Plage $$$$** *Belle Mare, tel: 402 2600, fax: 402 2626, <www.bellemareplagehotel.com>*. Large, well-established hotel that has benefited from a major 2003 refurbishment. Luxurious villas with private plunge pool or standard rooms are set in lush gardens with swimming pools and sea views. Free watersports, dive centre, mini-club for 4–12 year olds, two championship 18-hole golf courses, several à la carte restaurants and intimate bar provide everything you need for a beach-activity holiday.

**Domaine du Chasseur $$$** *Anse Jonchee, Vieux Grand Port, tel: 634 5097, fax: 634 5261, <www.dchasseur.com>.* Rustic, comfortably furnished thatched-roof lodges in the heart of a former hunting estate evoke an atmosphere of bygone Mauritius. Great walking trails on steep hills bounded by forest and panoramic views of Grand Port from the restaurant. Quad-biking, jeep safaris, hunting and helipad.

**Hotel Bougainville $** *Trou d'Eau Douce, tel: 480 2206, fax: 480 2432, <www.apavou-hotels.com>.* Go for the personal attention rather than a prestigious address at this homely haven where you can use the same beach as much grander hotels in the area. Simply furnished rooms, swimming pool, intimate restaurant and bar.

**Le Preskil $$** *Pointe Jerome, Mahebourg, tel: 604 1000, fax: 631 9603, <www.lepreskil.mu>.* Superb location with views of Lion Mountain and Île aux Aigrettes Nature Reserve. Popular with groups, being only a 15-minute drive from the airport. Garden rooms and sea-facing cottages in warm colours contrast with a trio of powdery white beaches . For the ultimate in privacy, try a couple of nights at the hotel's serviced eco-lodges, L'Exil or Andrea, set in stunning locations in the south.

**Residence $$$$** *Coast Road, Belle Mare, tel: 401 8888, fax: 415 5888, <www.theresidence.com>.* An east-coast celebrity haunt in a spectacular ocean-front setting. The focus is on tranquillity and well-being in the magnificent spa. Décor is colonial with lots of stone and thatch; the freeform pools emphasise a grand style.

**Le Tropical $$** *Trou d'Eau Douce, tel: 480 1300, fax: 420 2302, <www.naiade.com>.* This all-inclusive option managed by the

Naiade group attracts a predominantly French and British clientele. Pleasant, laid-back atmosphere with small swimming pool and bar. The buffet restaurant overlooks a narrow beach where there is a boathouse.

## THE SOUTH

**Les Ecuries de la Vieille Cheminee $** *Chamarel, tel: 686 5027, fax: 686 1250, <www.ecuriecheminee.com>.* High in the Chamarel mountains and close to the Coloured Earths, these charmingly rustic self-catering chalet bungalows offer a chance to explore rural Mauritius. Opportunities for horse-riding and trekking, as well as dining in nearby village restaurants. A two- or three-day stay here makes an unusual alternative to the usual sun, sea and sand.

**Heritage Golf & Spa Resort $$$** *Bel Ombre, tel: 601 1500, fax: 601 1515, <www.veranda-resorts.com>.* Mauritius's first all-inclusive luxury resort offers not just meals and branded international drinks but daily spa treatments too, access to 18-hole golf course, a host of water and land sports plus a full-day tour with lunch. Distinct Creole-African theme with large thatched-roof restaurants and bars, two fine pools and mini-clubs for young children and teenagers.

**Mövenpick Resort & Spa $$$$** *Bel Ombre, tel: 623 5000, fax: 623 5001, <www.moevenpick-hotels.com>.* With a subtle blend of Moorish and Dutch-Portuguese architecture, this is a stylish beachside escape for the discerning traveller. There's a state-of-the-art spa, an atmospheric Arab-style bar-cum-night-club and four swimming pools.

**Telfair Golf & Spa Resort $$$$** *Bel Ombre, tel: 601 5500, fax: 601 5555, <www.letelfair.com>.* This unique masterpiece of grand colonial-inspired architecture transports guests to an atmosphere of elegance and calm. Luxuriant gardens, three fine restaurants (one with show kitchen), colonial bar, mini-club, 18-hole golf course and spa. Guests can alternate between swimming in the lagoon and exploring the undulating hills of the Bel Ombre Nature Reserve.

## THE WEST

**Dinarobin Hotel Golf & Spa $$$$** *Le Morne Peninsula, tel: 401 4900, fax: 401 4901, <www.dinarobin-hotel.com>.* A tranquil and spacious chalet-style complex in an isolated position at the foot of Le Morne Peninsula, fronting a magnificent beach. Relaxing Clarins spa, mini-club, choice dining and access to facilities at sister property, Le Paradis, next door.

**Le Paradis $$$** *Le Morne Peninsula, tel: 401 5050, fax: 450 5140, <www.paradis-hotel.com>.* A haven for beach and nature lovers that includes international celebrity sportspeople on its guest list. The resort includes a championship 18-hole golf course, and offers deep-sea fishing, scuba diving, mountain biking, mini-club for 3–12 year olds and lively nightly entertainment.

**Sands Resort $$$** *Wolmar, Flic en Flac, tel: 403 1200, fax: 453 5300, <www.thesands.info>.* Discreet, serene and sophisticated beach hotel with wonderful views of the Tamarin Mountains. Ideal for empty nesters and honeymooners since it operates a child-free policy, although babies are welcome. Fine restaurant and huge pool.

**Sugar Beach $$$$** *Wolmar, Flic en Flac, tel: 453 9090, fax: 453 9100, <www.sugarbeachresort.com>.* Cool, white and spacious hotel reminiscent of colonial times, but with all mod cons. Particularly lively at night when entertainment shows are held around the pool. Enjoy a drink in the palatial 19th-century-style sugar plantation manor house. Guests can also use the casino and bars at the adjacent sister hotel, La Pirogue.

**Tamarin Hotel $$** *Tamarin Bay, tel: 483 6927, fax: 483 6581, <www.blue-season-hotels.com>.* Thorough 2004 refurbishment has given this 30-year old hotel a trendy art deco atmosphere. Close to the village, live jazz on Thursday evenings and a great location for body surfing. Cinema, mini-club, Zen spa, long rectangular pool for serious swimmers and boathouse.

**Villas Caroline $$** *Coast Road, Flic en Flac, tel: 453 8411, fax: 453 8144, <www.caroline.group.com>*. Attractive, well-maintained complex overlooking a brilliant white spit of sand within walking distance of restaurants and bars. Superb dive school and a wide range of water sports.

## PLATEAU TOWNS

**Gold Crest $** *Route St Jean, Quatre Bornes, tel: 454 5945, fax: 454 9599*. Comfortable, long-established 59-room hotel popular with short-stay visitors and those looking for an inexpensive town base. Convenient for shopping, and there are plenty of buses to Port Louis and Flic en Flac beach.

## RODRIGUES

**Cotton Bay Hotel $$** *Pointe Coton, tel: 831 8001, fax: 831 8003, <www.cottonbayhotel.com>*. Comfortable billet in superbly isolated beach location. Great diving right on the doorstep and access to glorious walks.

**Escale Vacances $** *Fond La Digue, Port Mathurin, tel: 831 2555, fax: 831 2075*. Stay in a cosy family atmosphere only a five-minute walk from the centre of town at this Creole-style hotel, which has an excellent restaurant.

**Morouk Ebony $$** *Pate Reynieux, Port Sud-Est, tel: 832 3351, fax: 832 3355, <www.mouroukebonyhotel.com>*. Attractive bungalow-style accommodation in cliff-top location with boathouse, dive school and kite surfing.

**Pointe Venus $$** *Pointe Venus, tel: 832 0104*. Delightful hotel on the headland, with lovely ocean views, a swimming pool and small spa, and a casual restaurant. Comfortable air-conditioned rooms and a traditional Rodriguan welcome.

## Recommended Restaurants

Restaurants in Mauritius, with few exceptions, are more popular at lunchtime than in the evening, when service tends to be slow and atmosphere often lacking. Lunch is normally taken from noon to 1.30pm and dinner from around 6.30pm to 7.30pm. In Mauritius, reservations are rarely needed except on Friday and Saturday nights at the more upmarket restaurants and hotels. In Rodrigues it is better to order lobster and seafood in advance. In general, restaurants offer a wide range of quickly prepared food but if you don't know what to order ask for *gadjacks* or appetisers before deciding on your main meal. For the budget-conscious there are plenty of rice- and noodle-based dishes.

The price categories below indicate the cost of a meal for two with soft drinks or beer (imported alcohol can double or even treble the bill). Menu prices do not always include 15 percent VAT, so check first. Tipping is discretionary.

| | |
|---|---|
| $$$$ | over R1,500 |
| $$$ | R1,000–R1,500 |
| $$ | R500–R1,000 |
| $ | below R500 |

## PORT LOUIS

**Black Steer $$** *Caudan Waterfront, tel: 211 9147.* Modern and minimalist décor in this smart air-conditioned restaurant, which specialises in great steaks, fish and chips, and Mediterranean cuisine. Good service and excellent presentation. The upstairs terrace gives views over the harbour.

**La Bonne Marmite $** *18 Sir William Newton Street, tel: 212 2403.* Crisp white tablecloths and air conditioning complement the Creole dishes at La Bonne Marmite, a popular lunchtime venue of Port Louisiens and tourists alike.

**Café du Vieux Conseil $$** *rue de Vieux Conseil, tel: 211 0393*. Popular with expats and members of the business community, this hideaway café, which is situated across from the Museum of Photography, retains a casual colonial atmosphere in a tree-shaded courtyard carefully concealed from the cacophony of town. The service is smart and the menu consists of tasty European and Creole dishes.

**Dolce Vita $$** *Domaine les Pailles, tel: 286 4225*. Enjoy a swim in the open-air pool and then tuck into the large portions of tasty pizza or pasta that are served at this casual Italian restaurant, located just a short drive south along the motorway from Port Louis.

**La Flore Mauricienne $$** *10 Intendance Street, tel: 212 2200*. La Flore Mauricienne is housed in Port Louis' original meeting place, dating back to the 19th century. This is a perfect pit-stop for a drink or two while people-watching from the terrace. For air-conditioned comfort, try the restaurant where *poisson vindaye* (spicy fish curry) is a local favourite.

**Namaste $$** *CaudanWaterfront, tel:211 6710*. Sophisticated Indian cuisine is served in this first-floor restaurant. There is an intimate atmosphere in the evening, but it is also good for lunch. Closed Sunday lunchtime.

**Restaurant Canton $** *15 Rue Emanuel Anquetil, tel: 242 2164*. This long-established restaurant does a roaring trade at lunchtime. Fast service, eclectic décor and good range of Chinese fare. Open daily. Last orders for evening meals at 7.30pm.

**Rose des Vents $$$$** *Labourdonnais Waterfront Hotel, tel: 202 4000*. Soft jazz and romantic harbour views conspire to tempt diners to blow the budget on champagne and a sumptuous seafood platter, which are just some of the gourmet delights on offer at this restaurant within the Labourdonnais Waterfront Hotel. Work off the excess with a gentle stroll around the harbour. Open for lunch and dinner. Closed Sunday.

## THE NORTH

**Café Muller $** *Grand Baie, tel: 263 5230*. This charming family-run German coffee shop tucked behind the main coast road is noted for authentic *stollen*, salads and snacks. Lovely garden setting with tropical atmosphere. Closed evenings.

**Cafeteria Pereybere $** *Coast Road, Pereybere, tel: 263 8539*. Long-established beach café, perfect for people-watching. Serves excellent Chinese and Creole food, including the local speciality, *poisson gingembre* (fish with ginger).

**Café Vanille Chocolat $** *Richmond Hill Shopping Complex, Grand Baie, tel: 269 1628*. Delightful coffee shop and ideal stop for a snack after shopping in Grand Baie.

**Chez Ram $** *Coast Road, Grand Baie, tel: 263 8569*. One of the few restaurants in the area that is always buzzing with tourists and locals. Typical Mauritian cuisine served by the welcoming owner and staff. Closed Wednesday.

**Coco de Mer $$** *Coast Road, Trou aux Biches, tel: 505 0240*. Enjoy Seychellois specialities, such as fish curry in coconut milk, in this simple, brightly decorated restaurant. Dishes are cooked to order, so be prepared to wait. If you can't endure the delay, then try the 'eat as much as you like' buffet on Saturday evenings. Reservations recommended.

**Don Camillo $$** *Grand Baie, tel: 263 8540*. Probably the best Italian restaurant in Grand Baie, next door to the Banana Bar. Don't be put off by its location beside the Caltex Petrol Station. Crisp tablecloths, candlelight, excellent service and consistently large portions of seafood, pizza and pasta.

**Le Fangourin $$** *Beau Plan, Pamplemousses, tel: 243 0660*. Overlooking lawned gardens, this charming restaurant is well placed as a lunch stop if you are visiting L'Aventure de Sucre Museum. Serves extensive Creole and European fare, and is renowned for delicious desserts using local speciality sugars. Open daily noon–5pm.

**Happy Rajah $$** *Royal Road, tel: 263 2241.* A hot favourite for authentic Indian food, with a terrace on which to dine or drink, and great jazz playing in the background. Good range of vegetarian and meat dishes, and accommodating staff. Try the selection of naan breads with vegetable *makhanwala*. Decent coffee and Indian desserts served. Closed Sunday lunchtime.

**Ritz Gentlemen's Club $$$** *Baie du Tombeau, tel: 247 4979.* For a tastefully erotic dining experience, which includes nimble pole-dancers as part of the act, men (and accompanied ladies) should head along the coast road for a wide-ranging menu reflecting Creole, Chinese and Indian cuisine. Open daily till late.

**Souvenir Snack $** *Coast Road, Trou aux Biches, tel: 265 7047.* Across the road from the police station and popular with beach-goers for a casual drink or snack. Sit beneath shaded wooden tables and tuck into chop suey, fried noodles or fish and meat curries. Open all day.

**Tante Athalie $$** *Pamplemousses, tel: 770 9792.* Named after the family maid who left behind some secret recipes, this quirky little restaurant has vintage cars in the garden and serves genuine home-cooked food only. Try the typical *rougaille*, rice, lentils and *bredes* (greens). Open for lunch only.

**Wakame $$$** *Royal Road, Pointe aux Canonniers, tel: 263 9888.* Authentic Japanese cuisine is served in this modern upmarket restaurant. Watch the chef prepare your goodies in the open kitchen, or help yourself to sushi on the conveyor belt. One of the better restaurants in the area, popular with ex-pats and worth splashing out for. Closed Sundays.

**Wangthai $** *Coast Road, Pereybere, tel: 263 9331.* Try the deliciously fragrant Thai cuisine, such as steamed crab and noodles or fish in tamarind sauce. Good-value family-run restaurant. Closed Monday.

## THE EAST

**Le Barachois $$** *Anse Bambous, Vieux Grand Port, tel: 634 5643.* Rustic dining experience with private alcoves surrounded by sea and mountains. You can enjoy a walk along a nature trail through mangrove plantations or take a dip in the pool. The seafood menu of the day tends to be expensive, but there is a varied à la carte menu.

**Chez Manuel $$$** *St Julien Village, Union Flacq, tel: 418 3599.* There's a nice buzz and pleasant service in this restaurant, which has lots of dining alcoves in a garden setting. Not cheap, but if you're staying on the east coast, dining at Chez Manuel is well worth the taxi fare to get there. Specialities include Chinese and Creole food, grills and seafood. Open for lunch and dinner. Closed Sunday.

**Le Four a Chaud $** *Route Royale Maho, Trou d'Eau Douce, tel: 480 1036.* Facing a 19th-century lime kiln on the Trou d'Eau Douce coast road, this upstairs restaurant specialises in seafood and Creole fare. Closed Saturday evening.

**Le Jardin de Beau Vallon $$$** *Beau Vallon, Mahebourg, tel: 631 2805.* This 100-year-old colonial house was rescued from rack and ruin by the present owners, who have faithfully restored it to its former glory. The shaded dining veranda, wooden floors and antique furniture reflect a bygone era. Surrounded by lush gardens of tropical fruit and trees, it's the place to enjoy Creole specialities such as octopus and green pawpaw curry. Good wine list, excellent service and private parking area. Open daily. Reservations recommended.

**Monte Carlo $** *Mahebourg, tel: 631 7731.* This simple eatery overlooking the bus station serves Creole, Chinese and Indian cuisine.

**Le Panoramour $$$$** *Anse Jonchee, Vieux Grand Port, tel: 634 5097.* This rustic restaurant occupies a wonderful spot atop a steep hill on a large hunting estate, giving magnificent views inland towards the hills and over the lagoon to the reefs at Grand Port, where the French and British fought it out in a naval battle in 1810. All produce is sourced from the estate, including the wild boar, venison and duck featured on the menu. Open daily for lunch, but do reserve for dinner.

**Symon's $$** *Pointe de Flacq, Belle Mare, tel: 415 1135*. It's well worth forgoing your hotel restaurant to come to this pleasant place where you can enjoy local food in a local setting. Seafood, Creole and Chinese food served inside or on the terrace. Closed Sunday.

## THE SOUTH

**Le Batelage $$** *Souillac, tel: 634 5643*. A former warehouse right on the banks of the Savanne River has been converted into an attractive restaurant. The menu offers both European and Creole dishes, and the service is generally unhurried. The laid-back atmosphere changes when tour groups arrive.

**Le Chamarel $$$** *La Crete, Chamarel, tel: 483 6421*. Rustic-style restaurant offering typical Mauritian cuisine on gorgeous hillside setting overlooking Ile aux Benitiers  and the lagoons of the southwest. Popular lunch stop for tour groups exploring the nearby Chamarel Coloured Earths. Open for lunch noon–3pm. Closed Sunday.

**Chateau Bel Ombre $$$$** *Bel Ombre, tel: 623 5622*. This upmarket restaurant occupies a colonial house in a spectacular setting bordering a golf course. Enjoy an informal lunch of venison or palm-heart salad or opt for a romantic soiree of gourmet dining. Extensive wine list. Closed Sunday. Reservations recommended.

**Green Palm $** *Coast Road, Riambel, tel: 625 5016*. Family-run simple eatery near Riambel beach specialising in authentic Creole dishes and seafood.

**The Hungry Croc $$** *La Vanille, Reserve des Mascareignes, Rivière des Anguilles, tel: 626 2503*. Feeling hungry after watching the crocs feed in this nature park? Then get your own back and tuck into a crocodile steak. It tastes remarkably like chicken, but the less-adventurous can opt for the croc-free *croque monsieur*.

**Le St Aubin $$** *Rivière des Anguilles, tel: 626 1513*. Step back in time at this handsome 19th-century plantation house on the A9, 5km (3 miles) northeast of Souillac. Enjoy a leisurely lunch of Creole dishes on the open veranda overlooking the lovely gardens. Both house and restaurant are popular with tour groups exploring the tea route. Reservations essential.

**Varangue-sur-Morne $$$** *Chamarel, tel: 483 6610*. Fabulous lunch location overlooking undulating cane fields with views of Benitiers Island. Timber stairways lead down to a charming restaurant specialising in Creole and European fare. Ideal if exploring the Black River Gorges. Popular with tour groups, so you should book ahead.

## THE WEST

**Le Bistrot du Barachois $$** *Route du Barachois, Tamarin, tel: 483 8735*. Fashionable hang-out with pleasant outdoor terrace at the back. Serves European and Creole food. The Lounge next door is a trendy pub-cum-disco. Closed Sunday and Monday.

**Domaine Anna $$$$** *Morcellement Anna, Flic en Flac, tel: 453 9650*. Upmarket Chinese food in this huge circular restaurant built from local stone. For romantic dining, ask for a private waterside pavilion. Specialities include seafood with palm-heart salad and steamed fish and ginger. Closed Mondays.

**Jac's Kitchen and Bar $** *Ruisseau Creole, Black River, tel: 483 8000*. Try the fresh croissants and coffee or grab a *croque monsieur* in this alfresco eatery after a spot of retail therapy in the nearby designer shopping complex. Open till late.

**Ocean Restaurant $** *Flic en Flac, tel: 453 8627*. Across the road from the public beach, this large Chinese restaurant has an extensive menu. Busy at weekends so best to book. Closed Sundays.

**Pavillion de Jade $$** *La Preneuse, tel: 683 6151*. This atmospheric Chinese restaurant on a first-floor terrace opposite the entrance to Black River National Park is an ideal stop before or after a long walk.

**Riverland's Café $** *Le Barachois Estate, Tamarin, tel: 483 8091*. On the banks of the River Tamarin and part of the modern Riverlands Sports Complex, this trendy location provides all-day snacks and meals beside the pool.

## PLATEAU TOWNS

**Mon Repos $$$** *Belzim Estate, Trianon, tel: 465 8403*. This converted 19th-century colonial mansion hidden in the cane fields behind Trianon Shopping Centre is one of the plateau town's treasured lunchtime secrets. Diners choose from a menu of traditional Mauritian cuisine in an atmosphere of calm sophistication. As well as dining indoors, you can also ask for a private table to be set up in the garden. Closed Sunday.

**Le Pekinois $** *Corner of Royal Road and Ambrose Street, Rose Hill, tel: 454 7229*. Well-established Chinese restaurant that does a roaring trade at lunchtimes. Closed Monday.

**Pot de Terre $** *Pot de Terre Lane, Curepipe, tel: 676 2204*. Right in the heart of town opposite the Monoprix Supermarket, this simple eatery is a popular choice with both locals and tourists. Try the daily specials or opt for a filling baguette.

## RODRIGUES

**Le Capitaine $** *Johnston Street, Port Mathurin, tel: 831 1581*. Cheap, cheerful and welcoming establishment for seafood, chicken and the daily special.

**Paille en Queue $** *Duncan Street, Port Mathurin, tel: 831 1616*. Popular bolt-hole for Chinese fare and Rodriguan beans, maize, squid and seafood.

# INDEX